THE ONE THING

THE ONE THING

TO ACHIEVE LIFE-LONG FINANCIAL SUCCESS

Eric Reinhold

**Academy
Institute Press**

ISBN-13: 9780998146409
ISBN-10: 0998146404
Library of Congress Control Number: 2016954835
Academy Institute Press, Longwood, FL
This book reflects the views of the author, is being provided only as a general source of information and is not intended to be used as a primary basis for investment decisions, nor should it be construed as advice designed to meet the particular needs of an individual investor. Investment decisions should always be made based on an investor's specific financial needs, objectives, goals, time horizon and risk tolerance. Please consult with your financial advisor regarding the evaluation of any specific information, opinion, advice, or other content.

The author does not provide tax or legal advice. Consult your tax advisor or attorney regarding specific tax or legal issues.

Library of Congress Cataloging-in-Publication Data

Published by: Academy Institute Press

www.theonething.one
Eric@theonething.one

CONTENTS

ACKNOWLEDGMENTS

I n order of importance:

God - Trust in the Lord with all your heart, and do not lean on your own understanding. In all your ways *acknowledge* him, and he will make straight your paths. Proverbs 3:5-6

My wife, Kim – It took seven years of dating to get her to the wedding alter. Thank you for encouraging me during life's challenges and supporting my optimistic and sometimes unrealistic dreams, for over twenty-eight years.

My children, Kaylyn, Kara and Kyler – Joys of my life, without whom this book would have been finished ten years earlier. Any time with you is time well-spent.

My parents and siblings – Mom and Dad, Baron, Kerstin, and John. Thanks for helping me hone my humor and the importance of family.

Lastly, I would like to thank Ron Blue, for starting the company where I first began learning the foundational principals of good stewardship with the resources God provides.

PREFACE

"*Most people I talk to find the idea of reading a book on money concepts as appealing as going to the dentist for a root canal.*" With all of the books that have been written on money and finances over the years, can someone really summarize the American Dream of retiring worry-free, down to one thing? I believe so, but I can't actually say that. I wanted to title this book, "The One Thing to Retire Worry-free," but, unfortunately (or fortunately), rules in the financial services industry prevent me from making promises. Compliance interprets these rules and supervision enforces it. In English that means that I'm not allowed to make definitive statements, regardless of how true I think these statements are. I would label these red light statements or words. They would include; never, guaranteed, 100%, sure thing, if you do this then that will happen, and so on. One thing is too positive. Surely there is one person out there who will do the one thing and it won't work for them. Next, there is what I call yellow statements or words. These are ones you can say, but they are going to have a bunch of qualified statements after them, just to make sure you don't take them as red statements. Generally these are concepts about asset allocation, diversification, and the stock market going up over the long-term, and so on. You will see these throughout my book. Lastly, there are green statements and words. These are the statements or words that I can use freely because they don't promise anything nor are they definitive. You know, essentially no help at all. These would include; maybe, possibly, you might, you may find, sometimes, and other wishy-washy terminology.

The legal community and politicians use these terms all the time because it gives them a way out of any situation.

If I sound sarcastic, it's because I am. It's a gift I was born with. My pastor preached on spiritual gifts once, but this one wasn't on the list. I believe God gave it me, because it usually makes people laugh. Although I'm pretty sure my compliance department thinks it came from Satan.

In this book, not only am I going to provide you with my one thing, but I'm also going to attempt to do the impossible. Most people I talk to find the idea of reading a book on money concepts as appealing as going to the dentist for a root canal. In fact, as I was seeking a publisher years ago to publish my children's fantasy novels, I had several ask me to write a finance book. My comment to them was, "I do that for a living. I'd like an escape in my free time to write something else." My decision to write a financial book now is based upon several self-imposed requirements. It has to have concise points, which anyone can put into action and it has to be entertaining. There's nothing I like better than reading a book that provides actionable advice while also making me laugh.

So what qualifies me to write this book?

I have been in the financial services industry for over twenty-two years. I've been compensated in the three main capacities: as commission-only, fee-only and as a fee and commission advisor. Prior to entering the private sector, I graduated from the U.S. Naval Academy with a B.S. in Economics and served five years as a Naval Officer. For my service selection, I chose to go into the Supply Corps so that I could be in the business side of the Navy. My jobs onboard ship were as both the Food Service Officer, essentially running four restaurants, and Disbursing Officer, which entailed payroll, currency exchange, and cashing checks. After my three years at sea, I was detailed back to Annapolis and served as the Midshipmen Financial Advisor. While on shore-duty at the Naval Academy, I went to night school at the University of Baltimore and completed my MBA. In addition, during the first five years of my financial planning career, I became a CERTIFIED FINANCIAL PLANNER™ certificant. This entailed a two year process, culminating in a two day exam.

When I mentioned the length of time I have been in practice as a financial advisor, there are several important aspects to that fact which will come out in numerous chapters. First, I have been through the emotions of both the good years in the stock market and the down years. 2008 is only the most recent time that fear ran rampant among investors, but 2000, 2001 and 2002 also had the markets dropping double digits, three years in a row. 1994, my first year out of the military and in financial services was very challenging in the bond markets. And while I was only an individual investor, I remember Black Monday in October 1987. Second, I have observed the many changes within the financial services industry over this time period, along with how firms and advisors have adjusted to it with their recommendations to clients. I hope to pass along my experience to you.

Are you ready for the "One Thing?"

In addition to my extensive finance and military experience, I've been married for over twenty-six years and have three children in various stages of college or graduated. Many of the navy, marriage and parenting stories I tell and relate to financial concepts are humorous now, but at the time they were a blend of fear, excitement, trepidation and anticipation. Lastly, while I am well aware of the rules for proper writing, I am putting my thoughts down on paper like we would be having a conversation in person. As a matter of fact, much of this book was written while enjoying a cup of coffee at my favorite bagel shop. If you don't have a cup of coffee in your hand, or you don't like coffee, picture yourself sitting down in a comfortable chair or couch with your favorite beverage. We'll have an informal conversation on serious topics that will affect you and your family, but hopefully laugh a little along the way. Now, as Admiral Farragut so famously shouted at the Battle of Mobile Bay, *"Damn the torpedoes, full speed ahead!"*

CHAPTER 1

WHAT IS THE ONE THING?

If you haven't seen the movie "City Slickers," you really need to watch it. Essentially, the plot boils down to Mitch (played by Billy Crystal), a middle aged, big-city, radio ads salesman and his friends Ed (Bruno Kirby) and Phil (Daniel Stern) having a mid-life crisis. They decide that the best birthday gift is to go on a two week vacation in the Wild West, driving cattle from New Mexico to Colorado. It is there that they meet cowboy Curly (Jack Palance), who not only teaches them how to be real cowboys, but also one or two other things about life in the open air of the west.

In one touching scene, Mitch and Curly are riding horses, side by side, as the weathered cowboy gives some sage advice.

Curly: Do you know what the secret to life is?

Mitch: No, what?

Curly: This *(He holds up one finger)*

Mitch: Your finger?

Curly: One thing. Just one thing. You stick to that and everything else don't mean squat.

Mitch: That's great, but, what's the *one thing*?

Curly: *(Smiles)* That's what you've gotta figure out.

As you start this book, you should be asking yourself, "What's the one thing?" And, if you're impatient like me, you may also be thinking, 'How do I skip through to find the answer?' I'm going to do something unconventional and give the answer to the question right at the beginning. Why? Because, while the answer is simple, carrying it out isn't.

After revealing the "One Thing," I'll spend the rest of the book discussing how to actually live it out in real life. To me there is nothing worse than reading the theoretical and then not having a game plan to actually enact it during the hectic pace of my everyday life.

In addition to providing practical application, I am going to attempt a more daunting task – making finances fun! I hope you enjoy the humor, anecdotes and stories I use to make my points.

From my bio and introduction, you know that I'm in the financial services industry. Therefore if you've read any financial literature you are certainly aware of all the **qualifiers**, small print, and *disclaimers* peppered throughout an article. I will provide my own qualification, in that while I might believe there is one thing you can do to ensure a positive retirement outcome 100 percent of the time, there's probably someone out there who can figure out a way to mess it up, even if they follow everything I say. Therefore I can't guarantee the *one thing*. But if you do follow this idea and the supporting points throughout my book, I believe you will be much better off. (I didn't make a guarantee there and if you are reading this then it means that the compliance department agrees).

So, what's the one thing?

"Spend less than you earn over a long period of time."

That's it? That's the big secret? Yes, and while it should be obvious that if you spend less than you earn you will have money left over, millions of Americans find themselves reaching retirement age with very few assets to add to their social security income.

Do you want *to achieve life-long financial success?* Do you want to be financially independent? Meaning you are free to continue to work in a vocation you love or leave a job you hate? Then spend less than you earn. You've probably heard this advice preached countless times, in different ways, and completely agree with it in principle. But you know how it goes. Saving money makes perfect sense, until you actually see something you want, and then the urge to 'get it now' can quickly overpower common sense.

In the heat of the moment, you don't think too much about the impact of a seemingly small purchase. But how much are you really giving up when you give in to small purchases? Here are a few ways daily spending can lengthen the amount of time you will spend working:

A cup a day keeps retirement away. The fewer dollars each paycheck that go to spending, the more you have left over to invest. No surprises there. But seemingly mundane daily expenses can reduce the size of your retirement nest egg. Just $5 per day on a coffee fix or other convenience food will cost you $1,825 per year or $54,750 over a 30-year career. That doesn't even include investment returns on those cups of java. For people who earn a $50,000 annual salary, that's an entire extra year of work just to pay for $5 worth of daily discretionary spending. If that worker spends close to 9 hours a day at work and commuting and works 20 days per month, that's 2,160 extra hours of dealing with work, boring meetings, incompetent bosses and the commute, just to finance a daily $5 purchase. I can hear you thinking, *"But Eric, it's only a cup of coffee. I want to have a life."* Life is full of choices and putting them into a long-term perspective may change your spending habits.

And just like the famous infomercials say, "But wait… there's more." If instead you saved that $5 per day, you could not only retire a year earlier, but perhaps much earlier than that due to the compound interest on that $1,825 you tuck away each year. Saving just $5 per day in a 401(k) will grow to $178,856 over 30 years, assuming 7 percent annual returns. (*This is for illustrative purposes only. Consumer experience will vary*). That's about three and a half fewer years you would need to work if you earn $50,000 per year. And if you also get an employer match of 50 cents per dollar contributed on that money, you will have $268,284 after 30 years, which is 5 and a half years' pay for the same worker. *(Groan) "Eric, for crying out loud, it's a cup of coffee."*

Budget doesn't have to be a dirty word. When your expenses are less each year, you can live well with a smaller nest egg in retirement. If you learn to live on $50,000 a year, (even if you earn much more than that) you only need to save up enough to cover the $50,000 per year in retirement, not enough to replace your current salary. In fact, living on $50,000 per year, working hard to earn more than that and saving the difference is one of the fastest ways to retire early. We'll talk more on this in a later chapter.

Prescription for less stress? A smaller lifestyle. A smaller monthly budget can also add to your peace of mind in retirement. When your standard of living is entirely dependent on what the stock or bond markets do, it's hard to not be nervous whenever valuations gyrate. But what if your spending is so low you can easily retire early and come up with the difference by working part time? Obviously you can still aim big and try to earn a large salary. But if an easier to find and less stressful job can cover your smaller lifestyle, then you don't have to worry as much about investment performance and can concentrate on enjoying retirement. A reduction in lifestyle can also allow you to take a more fulfilling job at reduced pay before you retire. I've had a number of clients who had the income/spending relationship right and decided in their fifties to make a career change and move from the fast-paced corporate job to a non-profit position which was less stressful and more personally fulfilling.

The One Thing. For some people, spending less is extremely hard. We all live in the same modern society that celebrates consumption. But think about what you are giving up whenever you click the "buy" button. Are years of working worth the extras that you will forget about after owning them for a while? In my opinion, the "One Thing" for success in personal finances is *spending less than you earn over a long period of time.* It sounds simple, but putting it into practice can be a challenge. The rest of this book is dedicated to helping you overcome that challenge.

CHAPTER 2

INTERVIEWING THE BOYFRIEND

Make a plan.

    A. *You were born to win, but to be a winner, you must plan to win, prepare to win, and expect to win.* Zig Ziglar[1]

    B. *Plans fail for lack of counsel, but with many advisers they succeed.* Solomon, Proverbs 15:22

    C. *Setting a goal is not the main thing. It is deciding how you will go about achieving it and staying with that plan.* Tom Landry

    D. *A good plan violently executed now is better than a perfect plan executed next week.* George S. Patton

    E. *Everyone has a plan 'till they get punched in the mouth.* Mike Tyson

These are some of my favorite quotes on planning. To have an effective plan you should:

(A) Make a plan, (B) Get input, (C) Set measurable goals, (D) Take action! and (E) Realize there are going to be obstacles and course corrections needed along the way.

There are a lot of people who call themselves "financial planners." Unfortunately, many of them skip the planning part and go right to product sales and gathering assets to invest. On the official Certified Financial Planner Board website (www.cfp.net)[2], they define financial planning as, "the process of determining whether and how an individual can meet life goals through the proper management of financial resources." The Board breaks the financial planning process down into six steps:

1. Establishing and defining the client-planner relationship
2. Gathering client data including goals
3. Analyzing and evaluating the client's current financial status
4. Developing and presenting recommendations and/or alternatives
5. Implementing the recommendations
6. Monitoring the recommendations.

The fields covered in the financial planning process typically include, but are not limited to:

- Financial statement preparation and analysis (including cash flow analysis/planning and budgeting)
- Insurance planning and risk management
- Employee benefits planning
- Investment planning
- Income tax planning
- Retirement planning
- Estate planning

As you can see, there is a LOT of planning to be done! It is the primary aspect of what I do on a daily basis. That said, I am also aware that planning, especially financial planning, is not something that is top of mind for those outside of my field of expertise.

In addition, personality can play a big role in whether you naturally gravitate towards planning in other areas of your life. For instance, if you were to interview any of my children, independent of one another, their commentary on my vacation planning would collaborate quite closely with one another.

Dad puts together a notebook before every trip; complete with daily (if not hourly) itinerary, MapQuest travel routes, hotel, car, and flight reservations (as needed) and pictures. There is even a cover to the notebook which summarizes the trip location and date.

Overkill?

Maybe to some. But while I build time into the schedule for spontaneous fun, I don't like leaving hotels, rental cars, and attraction tickets to chance. If you don't make a plan then you are forced to react to whatever life throws your way, with little or no preparation. This may be exciting to the thrill-seeker, early in life, but it's not something you want to be faced with when you want to retire.

When I think of lack of preparation, I am reminded of a cartoon I had framed of a man visiting a financial advisor. The caption read, "I'm retiring in a week and haven't saved a dime. Now's your chance to become a legend."

Be proactive in your planning.

What does it mean to be proactive? I'm not just talking about financial issues here. Let me give you an example that will hit close to home for all parents with daughters. Dads, you know how great your little girl is. Unfortunately, when they become teenagers, there will inevitably be another male figure who thinks your daughter is great as well. Do you have a plan? If not, the default is that one day, out of the blue (at least in your mind), there is going to be a conversation:

"Dad, Steve asked me out. Is it okay if he picks me up tonight at seven?"

"What? You're only fourteen,"

(*eyes roll*) "Dad? I'm sixteen."

"Oh yeah, uhh… who's Steve?"

"A boy from school. He's really nice."

(*hesitation*) "What did your mother say?"

"She said to ask you."

Does that sound like a plan?

Years ago I read a book by Dennis Rainey[3], in which he challenged father's to interview boys that wanted to date their daughters. I put pen to paper and jotted down a strategy consisting of three rules:

1. Encourage my son and daughters to go out in groups versus one-on-one.
2. The first time they could go out on a date one-on-one was at age 16.
3. Before a boy could go out one-on-one with my daughter they had to go out with me first.

Yes, you read point number three correctly. The response from the women in my house was very interesting. My wife was encouraged and comforted. I was being proactive on a big issue in our house and relieving her of a potentially stressful situation. My daughters were intrigued. One was coming up on 16 and the other was 14. At first I thought there might be negative push back, but surprisingly, they seemed to be relieved as well. First, it helped to get them off the hook in case someone asked them out that they weren't interested in. *"If you want to go out with me you have to go out with my dad first."* That can throw cold water on a creeper-guy's intentions. Second, they felt protected by their father. They knew that I would lay out the ground rules for dating my daughter ahead of time, so they didn't have to. In addition, it gave us some great discussion time after I came back from **the interview**.

So how did the process work out?

The first order of business for me was to get a yellow pad, find a quiet place to sit down, and then jot down both the questions I wanted to ask and the statements I wanted to make sure were understood. I have a list of my questions and statements in the appendix. A typical interview-date began after one of my daughters told me the name of the boy that wanted to go out with them and provided me with their family phone number. The conversation with the parent went something like this. "Hello, this is Eric Reinhold, my daughter and your son, go to school together and as you may know your son has asked her out on a date." *Quick acknowledgment.* "It's my policy that if my daughter wants to date a boy one-on-one, that I take him out first for breakfast or lunch to get to know one another. I was calling to see if it would be okay with you if I set something up with your son?" These calls were always well received by the parents of the boy in question.

In some cases the boy was someone I knew because I had seen or talked with him when my daughter went out with a group. In other cases when I picked him up from his house for breakfast or from school for lunch, it was the first time we had met. The first question I asked after a brief introduction in the car was, "So, Steve, what does dating mean to you?" And then I would shut up. For me, the key was to ask open-ended questions, so I didn't get yes or no answers. And then remain silent, no matter how uncomfortable the silence. I didn't want to bail him out.

By the time he finished, we were able to enjoy some awkward silence before arriving at the restaurant. The walk from the car into the restaurant gave him some time to gather his wits as we were seated and then went through the process of ordering. I would then move onto my second question. "So Steve, you and I both know my daughter is beautiful, what other things attract you to her?" Again, another open-ended question. For the boy that knew all the wonderful attributes of my daughter, this was a lay-up. But for the boy focused primarily on her physical appearance - beads of sweat appeared along with shifting nervously in his chair.

There were also blanket statements while looking him directly in the eye. "Steve, as long as you assume that every text, e-mail, chat, message, or phone call is seen or heard by me, then you'll be okay."

There were other questions and statements I've listed in the appendix, but I always liked to close with a summary statement. "Steve, whether you date my daughter once or fifty times, remember to treat her like you'd want someone to treat your future wife." While many sixteen year olds aren't thinking about marriage, I didn't keep it a secret that I was seventeen when I starting dating a newly sixteen year old girl, who later became my wife.

A lot of fathers joke about how they are going to be cleaning their gun when junior shows up to take out their daughter. I resisted the temptation to drop my concealed weapon permit on the table over lunch with potential suitors. But the reality is that most fathers aren't proactive in the vital area of raising and protecting their daughters. Having a plan is important, in both parenting and your finances. Being proactive with that plan is critical. But what happens when things don't go like you plan?

CHAPTER 3

DO YOU REALLY WANT TO MEET THE PARENTS?

Take Action!

In the 2000 comedy 'Meet the Parents', male nurse Gaylord 'Greg' Focker (played by Ben Stiller) is the trophy boy for disaster. Wanting to propose to his girlfriend, Pam (Teri Polo), the woman of his dreams, Greg learns that it is customary to ask her father's permission. However the cards are already stacked against him because his girlfriend's dad, Jack Byrnes (played by Robert De Niro) is an ex-CIA agent with an unhealthy case of paranoia.

The awkwardness begins when Greg shows up in an airport rental car, after flying to the potential in-laws for the weekend.

> **Jack:** "I'm just curious; did you pick the color of the car?"
> **Greg:** "Uh no, the guy at the window did, why?"
> **Jack:** "Well they say geniuses pick green."
> **Greg:** "Oh."
> **Jack:** "But you didn't pick it"

Jack has a plan. He wants to marry Pam. The question is, will Jack stick to his plan no matter what obstacles he may face? If you've seen the movie, you know the hurdles are great.

As noted previously, Tom Landry, the legendary Dallas Cowboys coach, is quoted as saying, "Setting a goal is not the main thing. It is deciding how you will go about achieving it and staying with that plan."

In working with clients over the past twenty plus years, I've had initial meetings where someone will say, "I had a plan done years ago," and they drop a large notebook on my desk. My initial thought is, 'I hope you didn't pay by the pound.' Having a plan is important, but it doesn't have to be overly complex and certainly doesn't have to be four inches thick. The key is in the recommendations and then working on those recommendations to completion. If asked, many attorneys will tell you that one of the biggest tragedies is a client paying for a great estate plan, but then skimping on paying the attorney to ensure that assets are titled correctly. The client has the best intentions of doing this themselves, but then life gets in the way and their assets are never retitled. The plan is worthless.

Are you prepared to not only make a plan, but put that plan in action?

When I came up with a dating plan for my daughters, I thought I was done. My reasoning was, 'These boys will listen to a semi-threatening six foot four father and follow my sage advice.' But what happens when the young lad thinks he knows better and wants to put the old man to a test? Further action may be required.

One of my daughters was taking a few summer courses to finish her four year degree in three and a half years. A bill came in the mail that I had a question about and I phoned the billing department at the college. The response I received was surprising.

"I'm sorry sir, we can't talk to you. We can only talk to the student."

"Really?"

"Yes, sir, it's due to privacy laws."

"That's interesting. So you don't want to talk to the person paying the bill?"

"I'm sorry sir, we can't."

"Okay, so you're saying I need to explain the situation to my daughter. She needs to call you. Then she needs to talk to me about the situation. And if I have further questions then we need to keep going through her?"

"Yes, sir. It's the law."

"Okay, but you do realize this is going to delay you getting paid?"

"I'm sorry sir, it's the law."

I'm not sure who proposed and got these laws passed, but I'm pretty sure they didn't have college kids. Regardless, privacy laws haven't made their way into the Reinhold household.

The names have been changed to protect the guilty, but there was one boy who passed the test of meeting with me, and had been dating one of my daughters for a while. As promised in our initial breakfast meeting, I was monitoring anything coming into our house from him. All seemed to be going well until my wife picked up a piece of paper off the floor that was a "love" letter from Allen to her. Two lines into his message it quickly went downhill, with him describing in detail some of his desires for greater 'physical interaction.' Only he used very descriptive terminology.

At that point I had a decision to make. Was my plan an idea or was I going to take action on it? If you know me well, you know the answer to this question. After talking with my wife, I walked over to my home copier and made three copies and starting highlighting the provocative parts. I think my wife's mouth was still aghast when I told her I was headed to Allen's house. In the car I put in a call to his house. His mother answered the phone.

"Hello, this is Eric Reinhold, I'm on my way to your house. Is it okay if I stop by?"

"Uhh… yes. Is everything okay?"

"I'll see you in a few minutes."

I knocked at the door and his mother answered and invited me in. I handed a copy to Allen and his mother. His father wasn't home. Then I said, "Allen, why don't you read this to your mother and tell me if it's something you should be sending my daughter."

The color completely drained from Allen's face.

There was silence as they both looked at the highlighted paper.

Allen's mother spoke first. Well, actually she yelled. "I did not raise a son like this!"

The moral of the story? Following through on a plan can entail more than you might first realize. No follow through = no plan.

In case you're wondering, the dating relationship ended that day.

CHAPTER 4

"PUNCHED IN THE MOUTH"

How do you handle adversity?

"*Everyone has a plan 'til they get punched in the mouth.*" Mike Tyson Depending upon your age, you might recall Mike Tyson in the early years as a heavy weight fighter. Knock outs were the norm. Mike didn't hesitate. From the opening bell he was across the ring throwing violent punches at his opponent.

Mike Berardino, a columnist of the Baltimore Sun Sentinel, had the opportunity to interview Mike Tyson in advance of the former heavyweight champion's appearance at the Seminole Coconut Creek Casino, where he performed his one-man stage show, "Mike Tyson: Undisputed Truth." He asked Tyson if he remembered the origins of that quote.

"People were asking me, before a fight, 'What's going to happen?'" Tyson said. They were talking about his opponent's style. 'He's going to give you a lot of lateral movement. He's going to move, he's going to dance. He's going to do this, do that.' I said, "Everybody has a plan until they get hit. Then, like a rat, they stop in fear and freeze."

What I like so much about the quote is that its application stretches far beyond boxing. It really has meaning in any area of life, whether the blow comes from a health issue, losing your job, making a bad investment, a traffic jam, whatever.

It's how you react to that adversity that defines you, not the adversity itself.

"Exactly," Tyson agreed. "If you're good and your plan is working then somewhere during the duration and before the outcome of that event you're involved in, you're going to get the wrath, the bad end of the stick. Let's see how you deal with it. Normally people don't deal with it that well."

This is a great analogy to financial planning. You put together a monthly budget and two weeks into it, an emergency comes up you didn't expect. The right-hook to the mouth. You prepared for it in training, but then life happens. Now what?

Something always happens.

It's not fair. You finally did a monthly budget. But life threw you a curve ball and messed up all your plans.

In the far recesses of your mind you hear the small quiet voice of your financial advisor saying, "Keep three to six months of living expenses in an emergency fund." At least I hope so. Imagine if you heeded that advice and put some money into a boring money market account for emergencies. It's the difference between throwing it on the credit card (more debt) and knowing, 'I have money set aside for situations like this.'

I remember the mid-eighties when I was a Midshipman at the Naval Academy. My girlfriend was in town and I wanted to be with her, not behind the walls of Annapolis. I was able to sneak out in the backseat of a friend's car. I had a great time that day. The problem was getting back in. A marine was guarding each gate. I was supposed to be back at 1800 hours (6 pm for you civilians). It was 2000 (8 pm). What now? This was an emergency. Time to go to plan B.

The normal secondary option is to try and climb over the wall. The lowest point in the wall at the Naval Academy is behind The Chapel, not too far from Gate 3. Midshipmen affectionately call this Gate 0. The only problem is that the administration is also very well aware of this well-worn exit and entrance by Midshipmen over the years. Many an Officer of the Watch has parked himself at this location, close to the end of liberty, to catch unsuspecting Midshipmen as they come over. I didn't want to challenge these odds, so I racked my brain for another option.

Oddly enough, my naval history class and Paul Revere's 'One if by land two if by sea,' quote came to mind. It just so happens that a friend's sponsor family had a business in channel navigation and rescuing boats on sandbars. Plan C. I contacted the sponsor and headed out on his boat. The interesting thing about the Naval Academy is that while there are three well-guarded gates you can enter by and the wall I mentioned covering the rest of the grounds, there are several miles of both jagged rocks and cement sea wall that borders the Severn River. Thirty minutes later, I was getting out of the boat onto a part of the sea wall by the football practice fields. I had the foresight to bring my official USNA PT gear with me and I jogged back to my room. Fortunately, exercise is encouraged at all times in the Yard!

The moral of the story? Things rarely go as planned, so plan for the best and prepare for the worst.

You and Your Health.

Check off the following statements you agree with.

- Cigarette smoking can cause cancer and is bad for your health long-term.
- You will feel better exercising 3-4 times a week.
- Drinking 6-8 glasses of water a day is good for you.
- Eating several servings of fruits and vegetables daily is good for you.
- Eating sweets and fast food in moderation or not at all is the healthiest.
- If you get at least 6-7 hours of sleep a night you will feel more refreshed.

You probably checked off every statement. If so, why are they so hard for most people to follow? The brain agrees yet our actions don't reflect what we say we believe. This is the difference between belief and conviction. According to the dictionary, a conviction is a firmly held belief or opinion. To be firmly held means that there needs to be action to substantiate that belief.

Chuck Colson, who was the Special Counsel to President Nixon and ended up spending seven months in prison, came out a changed person. He formed Prison Fellowship, which became the nation's largest outreach to prisoners, ex-prisoners, and their families. His changed outlook on life was reflected in how he lived and the convictions of his faith. This quote on Watergate and his faith expresses that conviction:

> *"I know the resurrection is a fact, and Watergate proved it to me. How? Because 12 men testified they had seen Jesus raised from the dead, and then they proclaimed that truth for 40 years, never once denying it. Every one of them was beaten, tortured, stoned and put in prison. They would not have endured that if it weren't true. Watergate embroiled 12 of the most powerful men in the world-and they couldn't keep a lie for three weeks. You're telling me 12 apostles could keep a lie for 40 years? Absolutely impossible. "[1]*

I remember during my First Class year at the Naval Academy (Senior Year), we all had to report to medical for a Commissioning physical. This was the biggie. If your vision wasn't 20/20 you couldn't choose aviation for your service selection, even if you reported to Annapolis with perfect vision as a Plebe. Other diagnosis could result in your not being fit for the Marines, SEALs, or Submarine duty. The Naval Academy's desire was for every Midshipman to be designated as an Unrestricted Line (URL) officer. This means that you are physically qualified for the Navy's combat communities.

I already knew my vision was bad, but I didn't want to fly, so that left submarines, the Marines, and surface warfare. As an economics major, I did have an interest in business and the business side of the Navy was the Supply Corps. To get in the Supply Corps, a Restricted Line (RL) billet, out of the Naval Academy you had to be considered not physical qualified. Other UL billets included Medical Corps, Dental Corps, Civil Engineer Corps, Judge Advocate General's Corp (the JAG attorneys) and the Chaplain Corps.

There were four doctors down in medical that day and the rumor among my classmates there that day, referred to one of them as Captain Hook, as in "hook you up." When my turn came up it wasn't with Captain "Hook," so I turned to one of my classmates and let him jump in front of me. When Captain Hook's door opened I jumped up and stepped in. The initial conversation went like this:

"So, what do you want to do?"

I replied, "I want to go Supply Corps."

His response, "Okay, let's see if we can find something."

The doctor's background was in cardiology and after his medical review he told me that he thought he heard something out of order, but couldn't be sure. My follow up was a trip to the Bethesda military hospital in Washington D.C. After the numerous test results came back, he sat down with me and let me know what he had found.

"It looks like you have a bicuspid aortic valve."

"What's that mean?"

"Well, you might have to have your valve replaced when you're seventy or eighty years old."

"What about for Service Selection?" I asked.

"Here are your choices. If I write it up one way you can be unrestricted line. But because of the length of time until I think it will affect you, if I write it up another way you can be restricted line. But once it's done you have to live with it."

My mother is a registered nurse and when I explained to her what the doctor said, she replied, "He can't do that." I believe the doctor was in one of those grey areas that allowed for light or dark grey. I didn't' argue with her, but I heard what I heard and told the doctor I wanted to be a Supply Officer. The next thing I knew I was part of the restricted line and was on my way to Athens, Georgia for 8 months of additional training after graduation into the Supply Corps.

I say all that to tie in two points. As a young, former football player, I felt indestructible and since the doctor didn't give me the conviction that it was a serious issue, I accepted the gift to get to do what I wanted in the navy, but didn't take the diagnosis seriously.

I served onboard the USS Yosemite (AD-19) as a Food Service Officer and Disbursing Officer for three years for my sea tour and then went back to the Naval Academy as the Midshipmen Financial Advisor on shore duty. When I left the service in 1994, I transitioned into financial services. The surprise came when I went to apply for a life insurance policy on myself and was Table Rated Z, which essentially meant I was uninsurable. Of course I was incensed. I was in the prime of my life, working out and running regularly. I called up the underwriter and asked if it would help if I sent in a video of me going through my workout regime? He responded that the only way a change would be made is if I went to a civilian doctor, told him my story and he changed my medical records to reflect a misdiagnosis. That is what I did, and a few months later I had a 15-year level term policy with a Preferred Plus rating.

This story ties together the two ideas of conviction and adversity and secondly, it provides a practical application for you to consider for your own financial security. The doctor who first diagnosed me wasn't very convincing for short-term consequences and even the long-term prognosis was iffy at best. When the civilian doctor changed my records to a misdiagnosis, my conviction that I had any serious medical issues was gone.

What is the most difficult thing you have every faced?

You might be wondering how my story ties in with adversity? If you fast forward seven years from 1994 to 2001 you get… the rest of the story.

At the beginning of September 2001, I was exercising regular and felt like I was in great shape. Then one day at the office I started breaking out in a sweat. I felt terrible that night and slept in another room in hopes of not giving a potential cold to my wife. The next morning I felt fine and went back to work. After lunch I started sweating again and the process repeated itself. A few days later I went in to my doctor. The evening news at the time had been dominated by stories about people being bit by ticks and getting fevers. I had ripped out most of the bushes around my house the previous week and thought this might be happening to me. I was also getting pain around my lower back. The doctor told me it was a cold and gave me pain medication for my back and sent me home.

9-11 occurred the next Tuesday, while I was driving up to Jacksonville, Florida for a few meetings with clients. Obviously those appointments were canceled as we all watched the news to try and understand what was happening. Personally, I was still dealing with my on again, off again, fever. I felt terrible by Saturday and made an appointment with a new doctor. As I sat in his office I began getting the chills. He listened to my heart and immediately sent me to the Emergency Room. It wasn't long before I was hooked up to IV's and checked into a room. A Transesophageal Echocardiograph (TEE) was done, which I will confirm is not a fun procedural test, and within a few hours the doctor came back with the results. She started out by confirming what I already had been told back in my commissioning physical - I had a bicuspid aortic valve instead of a tricuspid valve. The doctor then noted that I had endocarditis, a bacterial infection in my heart, which explained the fever, chills, sweating and flu like aches and pains. The next part was what floored me. The infection had affected my aortic valve to the point where it wasn't shutting properly anymore. In fact, sixty percent of the blood it pumped out was coming back into my heart, which had caused it to enlarge. If the situation wasn't fixed, it would result in me having cardiac arrest, most likely while exercising. I thought I was ready for the "fix," but I wasn't.

"We're going to have to insert a port into your chest so that you can give yourself intravenous therapy (IV), three times a day for a month to kill the infection. After that you'll need to have open-heart surgery to replace your aortic valve with a titanium one."

Adversity had arrived, front and center for me, at the young age of 37. I was fortunate, in that I was working in a financial planning group that had great medical coverage. Between the seventeen days in the hospital and almost three months at home, I was unable to work and my monthly income didn't miss a beat. Here are a few of the lessons learned from this experience that might benefit you.

It makes sense to look into whether a term insurance policy you are buying can be converted.

One of the best things I did after getting out of the Navy and getting my medical situation reversed was to buy a 15 year level term life insurance policy with a conversion provision. After my open-heart surgery, no one would write a policy on me. Eventually I had some Table C offers and even a Standard offer. In the 15th year, I converted the policy from Term to a Permanent policy at the same "Preferred Plus" rating I originally had. If you already have a term policy, check the terms to see if it is convertible and at the same rating.

Check what type of disability coverage you have in place.

Disability income typically covers up to 60% of your income through age 65. While there are benefits offered through the Social Security

Administration, it is extremely difficult to qualify for unless you are completely disabled. The next best place to get disability coverage is through your company, if they offer it. The best coverage is normally an individual policy; however, they are extremely expensive. I received short term benefits after the first week and my company was gracious enough to kick in the difference up to 100% of my salary. It wasn't listed as a benefit for me and I wouldn't count on your company doing the same for you.

Make sure your estate documents are up to date.

One of the most common weaknesses I see in a new client's financial plan is having no will or documents that are out of date. Acting as the trustee for my grandparents was quite the challenge. My grandfather was a Master Mechanic and owned a repair garage in upstate New York. Over the years he had purchased stock in a variety of companies and took ownership of the paper share certificates. He stored the certificates in a portable metal box. Every year as he travelled to Palm Beach for the winter, he carried the box in the car with him. Going through these certificates after his passing was quite the education. Some of the companies were household names. Those were easy. Others were mining company shares that were attractive for framing, but had long since gone out of business. Then there were the companies in between that had gone through several takeovers and name changes. It took months of research to track these shares down and determine if they were worth anything.

Today, most people hold shares in "street name" with their investment accounts. If your net worth isn't big enough to warrant a trust, then you may want to look into other options. You could set up a TOD (Transfer On Death) or a JTWROS (Joint Tenancy with Right of Survivorship) account. In both cases you would want to determine who the assets would be transferred to at death. In the case of the TOD account you could set that up with ownership by an individual versus the JTWROS, which is jointly owned.One of the differences is that if your assets are jointly owned then either person can make changes to the account during your life, while a TOD account focuses strictly on the transfer of assets to another person at death. These are discussions to have with your advisors since it is generally recommended to avoid probate if at all possible. Probate involves the court, attorney fees, and time to get assets moved from the deceased to the next rightful owner, as determined by a will, trust, or state law if none of those are in existence.

I am not an attorney and I do not write legal documents or provide legal advice; however, at the very least, I believe everyone should have a will. While I can discuss various trusts and other legal documents, you should contact an estate planning attorney to discuss the details of your situation. I used to have a humorous one-page document titled, "The No-will Will," that I would give to new clients. Sadly and truthfully, it laid out what could happen to your assets, based upon state law, if you died without a will. The worst potential issue was guardianship of your children. It's not necessarily who you think it would be. If you have minor children, determining who will be the trustee of your assets and who will be the guardian of your children is a must.

If you have certain items with sentimental value that you would like have go to a child, relative or friend, you can create an addendum to your will that lists all the items and who they go to. I've done this with my Naval Academy Class Ring and various collectibles.

In addition to a will, most attorneys will draft health care directives as part of a package of legal documents. These are the important legal documents that provide direction to your family and medical providers in the event of issues such as a coma, no brain activity, the inability to eat or breathe without a machine, and so on.

The benefits of a Trust.

Over the years I've seen the Federal Estate Tax Exemption amount bounce around from $1 million to $3 million, down to $0 for one year and then up to $5 million, with annual adjustments for inflation. Just because you are under the current limit doesn't mean you shouldn't have a conversation with an estate planning attorney about whether a trust makes sense for you or not.

One of the ways a trust can be beneficial is for the passing of assets to children, whether they are minors or not. I would also discuss, with the attorney, the wisdom of setting up trusts for each of the children for the assets to flow into. I sometimes joke with clients that this can protect the assets from, "In-laws and Outlaws, Creditors and Predators." Again, you have to discuss how to set the trust up properly, but think about your children inheriting what you've passed to them, only to have it taken away through a lawsuit due to a car accident they caused. A trust could protect the assets from litigation, creditors and even a nasty divorce.

Make sure your beneficiaries are up to date.

Most people think about updating their will and trust documents periodically, but there are other areas you need to remember to keep current. This is particularly true when you have major life events; like a death in the family or divorce. Beneficiary changes that can typically be made with a single page form include; insurance policies, annuities, IRAs and your 401(k) or other retirement plan at work. If you are divorced and remarried it will be a very awkward scenario if you die and your ex gets the check instead of your current wife and/or children.

CHAPTER 5

"EMERGENCY BLOW!"

What is and isn't an Emergency.

I f you're on a submarine, there are two things you definitely don't want – a fire or flooding. On a ship there is the potential to jump overboard. On a submarine you don't have that luxury. In case of emergency, the officer of the deck orders an emergency main ballast tank blow, also called an EMBT blow or just an *emergency blow*.

During an emergency blow, high-pressure air bottles, mounted inside the ballast tanks, exhaust their contents through large ball valves directly into the interior of the ballast tanks. This blasts 3,000 pounds per square inch air into the ballast tanks. The tanks "dewater" at a tremendous rate and within 30 seconds, the ballast tanks are dry, and the positive buoyancy rockets the submarine towards the surface at a 45 degree angle.

When it comes to your monthly finances, the reality is, everyone has issues that come up on a regular basis. It could be your air conditioner breaking down in the middle of summer. Or perhaps it's an unexpected health issue that requires surgery and you have a $10,000 deductible health insurance policy. What now?

A very common recommendation from financial advisors is to have 3 – 6 months of living expenses in an "emergency fund." One of the reasons for three to six months is in the event you lose your job and need time to find a new one. This should be enough time to get back on your feet and not have to start racking up credit card debt.

I have to confess, until a few years ago, I was very resistant to the idea of having a major emergency fund in cash. My rationale was, "I'm an investment professional, and I can have my investment portfolio be my emergency fund." I have had others say that they have a line of credit, cash value life insurance, or even high limits on a credit card, as their form of *emergency fund*. It took several key ideas to finally get me to the point of buying into a cash emergency fund:

1. You have to see the emergency fund as insurance not an investment. While life insurance is peace of mind for your beneficiary in the event of your untimely death, the emergency fund is peace of mind for you while you're living. For example, if a relative passes away unexpectedly and you need to buy an airline ticket to get there, you have some funds available.

2. See the emergency fund as a stress reliever. I have to admit that I didn't get it, until we had the first "emergency." In this case it was the AC going out. In the past I would have stressed out about putting it on a credit card and then having to pay it back. With my emergency fund I just paid it. No stress. I then took a few months to get my emergency fund back up to the level I started with.

3. Cash is King. When I had my investment account acting as an emergency fund, I was subject to the whims of the stock market on whether it ended up being a good idea or not. When the market was down and I had to dip into my investments, I had to take a loss. When you work out of cash you never have to worry about selling low.

4. Peace of mind for your marriage. Typically, one of you will be the maverick and the other will be more conservative, when it comes to money issues. While the maverick won't understand the need for a cash emergency fund, your frugal mate will have an uncanny sense of calm. Their sense of well-being is worth the minor potential gain you might get from the stock market.

I can't leave this topic without addressing what constitutes an emergency and what doesn't. How do you view the following?

Auto Repairs? Have you ever had a car that never needed to be repaired or tires that never needed replacing? No, so why are you surprised when you get a flat or the transmission blows? You should have a "Car Repair" line item in your budget and put cash into it monthly. If the repair is higher than the cash in your designated envelop, then you go to your emergency fund.

Christmas? This one is amazing. Every year December rolls around and people act like, 'Who knew Christmas would come in December, again?' Really? What would happen if you saved $50 to $100 a month in a Christmas envelope? I know one thing for sure. You would be in a much different place than the majority of Americans who dread opening their credit card statements in January. Instead of sucking the joy out of Christmas and giving, you can plan ahead and have a fun time being generous.

Once in a lifetime opportunities? Over the years I have learned that there is no such thing as a once in a lifetime opportunity. You may have a friend that calls you up and invites you to come along on a trip to Italy, where he has a free place to stay, but you have to take care of the $1,500 airfare, food, and transportation in country. If you have to put the trip on a credit card, I would say, skip it. Italy isn't going anywhere. But if you have $20,000 in an emergency fund, you have options. While this might not be an emergency and you weren't planning to go to Italy, so you hadn't saved up for it specifically, you can at least choose to go without debt and pay your emergency fund back over time when you return.

Annual Expenses? There are a number of annual expense items that you should be aware of and save for monthly, so that they don't become an emergency when they come due. These could include: annual property taxes, annual homeowners insurance, other annual insurance premiums, and house or car repairs, to name a few.

CHAPTER 6

THE DREADED "B" WORD

Why budgeting is important.

The *One Thing* I reveal in Chapter One is – **Spend less than you earn over a long period of time.** How can you spend less than you earn if you don't know what you're spending? The answer is - you can't. To succeed in finances and achieve financial independence, you must have a budget. *Eric, that's a pretty strong statement.*

Okay, is it an absolute? It depends upon what you mean by budget. I have clients that make a substantial income. At the same time it's in their nature to be frugal. So while they might not have a written budget they review on a regular basis, they naturally keep one. Before you jump on that train, let me tell you... that's not the norm. Some people are super human, but for the rest of us, let's focus on a proven blueprint for success.

Budget is not a four letter word, neither literally or figuratively, in my opinion. A budget is a tool to help you achieve your goal, in this case a confident retirement. In this chapter I want to provide you with some tools and guidelines to help alleviate the negativity that setting up a budget evokes.

Why do people hate budgeting?

That's simple. It's because we're Americans. We don't want anyone telling us what to do. Therefore, I'm not going to tell you that you have to do a budget. I'm going to explain the benefits and how to make it as painless as possible. Then armed with this you can decide that it's something

YOU want to do. As you've probably gathered, I'm a big movie fan. Like most of you, I grew up with Star Wars. Recently it has made a big comeback. Try using the Jedi-mind trick on yourself. Instead of, "These are not the droids you're looking for." Replace that with, "I know doing a budget is good for me."

Some of you reading this use other creative excuses:

"I'm too old to do a budget." A spin-off of, "You can't teach an old dog new tricks."

"Budgets are for people that don't have a big income."

"I'm too sophisticated to do a budget."

"I tried keeping a budget before. It doesn't work."

"I don't have enough time."

Enough already. I'm reminded of when I was a Plebe at the Naval Academy. On I-Day (Indoctrination Day), sometime between getting my buzz cut and getting my gear, I was informed of my five basic responses. These were the only ways I could respond to upperclassmen Plebe year, unless I was asked to explain further. The responses were: *Yes, Sir! No, Sir! Aye Aye, Sir! I'll find out, Sir! And No excuse, Sir!* So let me ask this again. **Why haven't you done a budget?**

I can hear you the words under your breath, **"No, excuse, Sir!"**

Now that we have that over with, let's get on to budgeting!

Since the goal is to spend LESS than you earn over a long period of time, let's start with the EARN part. For earning purposes, I am going to define it as take home pay. You obviously have taxes taken out of your pay first. After that most people have deductions, which may include your 401(k) or other retirement plan, health, life and disability insurances, and other benefit options. You can include these deductions in your budget if you like, but just make sure to add your pay back in if you do.

Now that you have the earning side of your budget sheet, you need to put together your expenses. The following is a standard budget sheet listing more items than you probably have, but hopefully it will help prompt you to remember all the areas you spend in monthly. Start filling in the easy ones first. Those are the fixed expense items that don't change each month, for example; auto insurance, mortgage or rent payment, pest, yard or pool cleaning services. Next, fill in the ones that vary slightly each month with your best average estimate. These would include items like, utilities, cell phone, and car fuel. The last budget items are the hardest. These are the categories that you have the most control over because you are determining how much you are going to spend. Items here would include, dining out, clothing, and entertainment.

SAVING	CHARITY	FOOD
Retirement	Tithe	Groceries
College Fund	Charity	Dining out
HOUSING	**TRANSPORT**	**UTILITIES**
First Mortgage	Gas & Oil	Electricity
2nd Mortgage	Repairs	Water
Real Estate Taxes	License	Cell Phone
Repairs	Car Fund	Internet
Assn Dues	Other	Cable TV
MEDICAL	**PERSONAL**	**PERSONAL**
Medications	Gifts	Child Care
Doctor Bills	Baby Items	Toiletries
Dentist	Pet Supplies	Cosmetics
Optometrist	Music/Tech	Hair Care
Vitamins	Subscriptions	Books
Other	Walk Around $ #1	Alimony
Other	Walk Around$ #2	Org. dues
Other	Child Support	
RECREATION	**INSURANCE**	**DEBT**
Entertainment	Life Ins.	Car paymt #1
Vacation	Health Ins.	Car paymt #2
Auto Ins.	Homeowners	Creditcard #1
CLOTHING	**INSURANCE**	**DEBT**
Adults	Disability	Creditcard #2
Children	Long-term care	Creditcard#3
Dry cleaning	ID Theft Ins.	Studentloan1
	Auto Ins.	Studentloan2

Take home pay_____ - (minus) Expenses_____ = Savings _____

The number in savings is the additional amount of money that you have discretion over to put towards short and long-term goals. I will dedicate separate chapters to discuss where to put your savings and how best to plan for your short and long-term goals.

People are funny creatures, in that they always want to compare themselves to everyone else. There's an app you can use that will compare what others have paid for a certain make and model of car in your area. This is supposed to reassure you that you don't pay more than everyone else. Of course my cynicism takes over and asks, "So why would I want to pay the average price of what everyone else probably overpaid for?" Regardless, even though I never presume to tell anyone how much they should spend in any given area, I am frequently asked what other people budget. With that in mind, here is a range of what others tend to spend out of their income, in each category:

Charity 10-15%	Food 5-15%	Savings 10-15%
Clothing 2-7%	Debts 5-10%	Transport 10-15%
Utilities 5-10%	Medical 5-10%	Insurance 10-25%
Personal 5-10%	Recreation 5-10%	Housing 25-35%

If you've never adhered to a budget before, I want you to treat it like a marathon not a sprint. The first few months will be a challenge as you possibly find out for the first time in your adult life what you are really spending versus what you thought. Now that you've put a budget down on paper, the harder part is actually following it. Here are some practical ways to instill some discipline in your life so that you can become more confident in your future retirement.

- Move from credit to cash
- Put every dollar into a line item on your budget
- Have a budget meeting every month
- Enjoy the freedom with no guilt
- Put something in the "Pocket Money" category

Let's explore these in a little more detail:

Move from credit to cash - In the internet age with check deposit by phone, debit and credit cards, and even the ability to purchase items by swiping your phone, this may seem archaic, but it works. When I first got out of the military, I went to work for one of the largest fee-only planning firms in the country. The President of the firm did a personal study on his own finances and found that over the course of a year he spent 23% less when he only used cash. The previous year he used credit cards and paid off the balance each month, but when he used only cash he spent less. Why is that? The reason is simple. When we spend cash, we feel the purchase. You can test this theory out one weekend when you have a little time. Get $100 in cash and go to the mall. When you buy that mocha-frappe-whatta-grande' at your local coffee shop, see how it feels to pay in cash instead of having them swipe your debit or credit card. Next, do some window shopping for a book or earrings. When you get up to the counter and have to part with Andrew Jackson or Ben Franklin, you might decide you'd rather keep your new found friends in your purse or wallet. Unlike swiping, which evokes no emotions, when you part with cash, you feel something.

Assign every dollar to a budget line – This means that you account for every net dollar you calculated by putting it in your budget. The fixed expenses are easy, so subtract them out first. The semi-variable ones come next because they will vary some from month to month. I would also include what money you are setting aside for short term goals at this time. You might be putting away $200 a month for that next car purchase in six years. Or even an additional retirement fund outside of your 401(k) that you maxed out at work. The last expenses are variable ones. These are the ones you determine with the remaining dollars and pay for with cash. At my house, we use the simple, old-fashioned, envelope system. At the beginning of the month my wife or I go to the bank, get cash and stuff our envelopes. For us they include: groceries, dining out, clothing, car repairs, pool and lawn chemicals, cosmetics/hair care (yep, none of that is for me), entertainment and most importantly walking around money for me and my wife (more on this later).

For *pool and lawn chemicals,* I might not spend anything for two months, but I still put my money in each month because I estimate what I'll need for the year and divide by twelve. Let me tell you, it's great going into the pool store and pulling out my envelope to pay in cash. I'm sure I'm the rare customer that does that, but I like not seeing the credit card add up. I only spend what I have in the envelope.

Groceries, dining out and entertainment can be huge variables in your budget. There are almost unlimited discretionary *wants* at Costco when you're roaming the aisles. All of a sudden you get the feeling that I *need* a new watch. I *need* that golf driver on sale. I *need* a six-pack of Multi-Vitamins. And it goes on and on. If I'm paying cash for groceries, I don't pick up unnecessary items, because it will be very embarrassing at the counter when I don't have enough cash and need to return the extra items because I shopped on an empty stomach. What happens when an envelope runs out of money? ***Warning*** don't panic! I can almost guarantee this will happen during the first few months of budgeting. Don't get discouraged. You can use it as a teaching tool if you have children. When we get to the 25th of the month and the dining out envelope is empty, we're eating at home until the 1st of the next month. Towards the end of the month you might hear this conversation around our house. *"Hey kids, is there any money in the entertainment envelope? No? Okay… we'll see that movie next Friday."*

Have a budget meeting every month – My wife and I meet each month for about 30-mintues to discuss the upcoming month's budget. Once you've done it a few times, it becomes easier. In fact, sometimes we have our budget meeting over our weekly Saturday morning bagel time at Einstein's. The focus each month is on what, if any, new items are going to be added or subtracted from the previous month's budget. If I get a bonus and my income is going to be higher that month, then what budget line am I going to put those dollars in?

Enjoy the freedom with no guilt – For some, budgets seem restrictive, but in reality it is very freeing. Consider this, how many times have you seen your significant other sneak in the house with a package, hoping you don't see it so they don't have to reveal how much they spent? Maybe you're that person doing the sneaking. Instead, what if you both decided ahead of time how much would be in the tool budget for the month and how much would be in the shoe budget? Now when either of you come home with a package there aren't any issues. You can blow it all in one day or over the course of the month. It doesn't matter. It's in the budget! To me that's freedom not restriction.

Put something in the "Walking Around Money" category – My favorite category in the budget is the "walking around cash," line item. Decide at your monthly meeting how much that will be. It's a budgeted item you can spend however you want. No questions asked. You might have an extra tool you wanted to buy that wasn't in the budget. Or you may have a hobby. I have three fish tanks in my home office. Sometimes my walking around cash goes towards a new fish or item for a tank. And the best thing is unlike some cell phone plans that don't have "rollover minutes," if you don't spend it all you can keep it and add to it next month. Unfortunately, this doesn't seem to happen to me. Believe it or not, my walking around cash is typically out by the 20th of each month!

I hope by now you understand that "budget," doesn't have to be a dirty word. In reality it is an outward expression of deep, inwardly held values and principles. What we do is a visible manifestation of how we think and what we really believe. If you give me your checkbook and calendar I'll be able to tell you pretty quickly what is important to you. A budget meeting every month helps to recalibrate our lives and make sure it is balanced. Especially when it comes to two people sharing a life together that may have come from very different upbringings when it comes to money and how it is saved or spent.

CHAPTER 7

INVESTING WITH MY HAIR ON FIRE!

The Tortoise and the Hare

You probably know Aesop's Fable about the Tortoise and the Hare. A boastful rabbit, who is quick on his feet, ridicules a slow-moving turtle. After a time, the tortoise grows tired of the hare's boastful behavior and challenges him to a race. The hare rapidly leaves the tortoise far behind and, confident of winning, takes a nap midway through the race. When the Hare awakes, he is mortified to find his competitor, crawling slowly but steadily, has arrived at the finish line before him.

Two quotes come to mind when I think about the tortoise and the hare. The first concerns the Hare and is from the navy fighter jet movie, Top Gun.

"You're not going to be happy unless you're going mach two with your hair on fire." Goose's wife to Maverick.

And the second is from the Bible and concerns the tortoise.

"Dishonest money dwindles away, but he who gathers little by little makes it grow." Proverbs 13:11

With investing, most of the time it isn't "dishonest" money that dwindles away, but money poured into companies that are speculative. My definition of speculative would be high risk companies that have one or more of the following characteristics: a penny stock (stocks selling below $5 a share), a company with no earnings and a high level of debt, companies in industries dependent upon FDA approval or technological advances which may or may not work.

I remember the early 90's, when I was a young naval officer and a DINK (dual income no kids). I was interested in the stock market and reading up on the hottest sectors. At the time, biotechnology was the rage. I read about companies that came out with fantastic new drugs, and then went through the requisite phases and trials, before presenting their findings to the FDA for approval. As I saw it, the key was to read up on companies in Phase One and Two, invest early while the stock price was still low, and then hold on until approval. Simple enough, or so I thought.

The question I should have asked myself is, how much can an individual really know about a biotech company and its wonder drug? I read reviews by supposed experts, but speculative stocks like these typically have terrible financials. There is little to no revenue and tons of money being spent on Research and Development (R&D). The headlines in various financial magazines all shouted about the huge profits in biotech, so I forged ahead. I jumped into a company that seemed like the best of the ones I had read about and was happy to see it move up over the following few weeks as each new and promising story came out. Then one Monday I was in the Wardroom, onboard our ship, which was still in port. I opened the Wall Street Journal (the internet wasn't up and running yet) and was shocked to see my company down 35%. An article in the paper described how numerous people had died during the clinical trials in Europe. That's definitely not something you want to have happen. Another company I didn't invest in, because the price was too high at over $300 a share, is now listed at less than $1, twenty five years later.

A decade later, you might recall the dot-com bubble that ended up bursting in March of 2000. The bubble grew as the new internet stocks soared. Initial Public Offerings raised substantial amounts of money, and that money was spent lavishly on $2 million 30 second spots for Super Bowl ads and elaborate corporate headquarters. Anything with a .com after its name seemed to make money. No one wanted to miss out. Everyone had a tip on the next big thing. I recall investing some speculative money I had set aside, in a company for $1 a share. A few weeks later it was at $2 and I sold it. I thought 100% profit was great. Within a week it was at $4, then a day later $7 and I finally jumped back in at $12, rode it to $24 and sold it again, only to see it peak at $32 a share a month later. Do you think I had any remorse at selling my one dollar shares too early? For a while, but within six months that company was out of business and worthless.

Both of these stories are examples of investing like a Hare or investing with your *hair on fire*. Here are a few things I learned from the experience:

- Greed is a strong emotion that can cause you to ignore good investing principles.
- For every one stock you hear someone bragging about, there are nine others they are embarrassed to bring up.
- The concept of diversification* (or not putting all your eggs in one basket) works well in industries with high growth stocks.
- Speculation is the same as gambling.
- Even if you get one stock right, making the wrong investments will typically pull your overall returns down and result in a worse return than being slow and steady.

*While diversification doesn't guarantee a gain or keep you from losses, it is a way to spread your risk among a number of companies and will typically reduce the overall volatility of your investments. A case in point would be investing in an Exchange Traded Fund (ETF) or sector mutual fund that invests in Biotechnology. Both of these investments are in the biotech industry, but instead of being invested in one stock, they are invested in over thirty. If one company in the investments goes out of business, you won't lose your entire investment.

What about investing like the tortoise?

There are time-tested investing principles that over a long period can provide you with the best opportunity to grow your assets and accomplish your goals. So why don't people follow them? The simple answer is, because they're boring. Like the tortoise and the hare, most people would choose the sports car over the mini-van. But if you have to choose one of them for the long-term, that will have the least amount of garage repair visits and be practical to transport more people and stuff, then you'd be smart to go with the mini-van.

Three investing concepts you can't go wrong with:

Diversification – We discussed this a little with the Hare. "Don't put all your eggs in one basket." Everybody knows that. I searched for the origin of this saying and the earliest account noted was in the sixteen hundreds. But then I recalled reading about a similar concept that originated quite a bit earlier. King Solomon wrote the following, sometime before his death in 931 BC. "Divide your portion to seven, or even to eight, for you do not know what misfortune may occur on the earth." Ecclesiastes 11:2 (NASB). Diversification helps to mitigate losses, but that doesn't mean it eliminates them.

The first level of diversifying in equity investments is putting your assets in more than one stock. This can be done through purchasing twenty or more individual stocks or more normally it is accomplished through purchasing a mutual fund. A typical mutual fund holds fifty to five hundred different stocks. On most days, some will go up and some will go down. At the end of the day, they are all revalued and the new price per share is listed. If a few of the stocks perform poorly for some reason or even go out of business, you have others to make up for it.

The next level of diversifying can be accomplished by investing in different asset classes. Asset classes include; U.S. Stocks, International Stocks, Emerging Markets, Bonds, Real Estate, Gold, and Commodities. Many of these asset classes can be further sub-divided. For instance small company stocks versus large company stocks or high yield bonds versus municipal or international bonds. If you ranked the best performing asset class each year, you would observe that there is not one that is at the top every year. If there was, everyone would invest in it and there wouldn't be a need for an advisor or advice on how to invest.

Dollar Cost Averaging – Everyone wants to buy low and sell high. That is easier said than done. One way to effectively budget, save and invest, all at the same time, is to dollar cost average (DCA). With DCA you determine how much you want to invest monthly and then set it up so that these assets are invested on the same date each month. If the price goes down in the fund then you purchase more shares. When the price goes back up, you purchase fewer shares, but your shares are worth more. By using this method, if you bought shares at $50 each, the first month, and then every month over the course of the year, and the share price dropped and then rose again ($48, $46, $45, $43, $40, $39, $42, $44, $46, $49), so that by the end of the year the price was back to $50, you would have an overall gain for the year. You would have an average share price of $45.16, with a current share price of $50. Since historically, the stock market rises over a long period of time, if you invest long-term then it is more likely that you will accumulate savings.

The earlier you begin investing, the better – Albert Einstein said, "Compound interest is the eighth wonder of the world. He who understands it, earns it… he who doesn't… pays it." When you invest your money, it makes interest, dividends, and grows over time. Then you make money on that money and the original principal. This concept works well in tandem with the DCA concept mentioned previously.

On my shore-duty in Annapolis, as the Midshipmen Financial Advisor, I frequently gave lectures to the students. It was gratifying to receive an e-mail this year, 22 years after the fact, from a Midshipman who had attended one of those lectures and put this principal to work. Essentially, I provided them with a chart showing how one Midshipman began investing $2,000 in a mutual fund, every year for six years, from age 21 to 26. The next midshipman waited until age 27 to start investing his $2,000 a year. Due to compound interest, the midshipman who started earlier would invest a total of $12,000 by the time he turned 27. He wouldn't invest another dime, but would allow this money to compound and grow, and would have $1,348,440 by the time he turned 65. The Midshipman, who waited until age 27, would have invested $78,000 ($2,000 a year from age 27 to 65) and his account would be worth $1,368,020 by age 65 – virtually the same.

If you are reading the above and wish you would have started at age 21, you have a few options. One, you can pout. Two, you can discuss this with your children or grandchildren and get them started early. Back in 1992, when I was teaching this the maximum annual contribution to an IRA was only $2,000. It has increased substantially, so the end result could be even better.

The good news is that it's never too late to start. If you're starting to invest later in life, you probably have a higher income. So attack your expenses by reducing them and divert at least 15% of your monthly income to your retirement investing.

CHAPTER 8

SKEPTICS 101

Are the BIG BOYS right?

I am frequently accused of being a skeptic. Whether it's a pastor preaching, a television news commentator, a Wall Street Journal article, a politician, and certainly anything on the internet, I'm not going to christen it *the truth,* until I do additional research and follow up myself. With that in mind, here is a contrarian view on asset allocation and the "buy and hold" strategy.

"You're in for the long-term, so don't worry about this temporary down market." Words to that effect are what you will hear from many financial advisors and TV pundits when your investment accounts are dropping. This can be both reassuring and frustrating. Reassuring from the standpoint that history has shown that if you stay in the stock market long enough, eventually your account value should recover. Frustrating because you may be wondering why you can't avoid some of the market drop by moving to cash or other investments that aren't highly correlated to the stock market.

As mentioned previously, typical asset allocation is the process of determining which percentage of a client's portfolio should be in stocks, bonds and/or cash, with the intention of maintaining that allocation for at least five years, barring some major change in your investment objectives.

What will not force a change in allocation is market activity (the ups and downs). In fact, proponents of static asset allocation see that as one of its major benefits. The discipline that holds the allocation to stocks at

60%, for example, while the market is going through the roof – or the floor – keeps clients from getting whipsawed as they try to chase the top-performing investments.

Cynical view #1 – Has asset allocation been over-hyped for the benefit of asset gatherers?

Asset allocation has been the standard operating procedure among financial planners for the past few decades. Although it is based on the work of economist Harry Markowitz, whose paper, "Portfolio Selection" was published in the Journal of Finance in 1952 and formed the basis of modern portfolio theory; it was not until the 1990s that the concept really took off.

The pivotal study that unleashed the trend was published in the July/August 1986 issue of Financial Analyst Journal. In "Determination of Portfolio Performance," Gary Brinson and colleagues concluded that 93.6% of portfolio returns can be explained by asset allocation policy.[1] Their analysis was brought about through the foundations of asset allocation theory with a body of work called the Capital Asset Pricing Model (CAPM) using beta as a measure of risk, which evolved into Modern Portfolio Theory (MPT) using standard deviation as a measure of risk. With this newfound "scientific" evidence, advisors could justify allocating a client's assets to stocks, bonds, and cash based on their risk tolerance and time horizon.

In the financial services industry, I describe "Asset Gatherers" as those who ask a potential investment client 10 to 15 risk tolerance questions and then, based upon their responses, recommend one of eight or so (asset allocated) model portfolios. These portfolios are managed by a third party and may even have automatic annual rebalancing. The advisor is then freed up to find the next client. Is it justifiable to question if this is the best investment platform for clients? Is it cynical to think that it might possibly be an easy process to sell people on?

Consider this.

In direct contradiction to the Brinson study, James B. Cloonan, chairman of the American Association of Individual Investors (AAII), had this to say about the idea of putting a certain percentage of your assets in bonds or stocks: "Which bonds, which stocks?" He said that if he's considering a portfolio that is 70% invested in an S&P 500® index fund and 30% in a bond fund; he can always find a 100% stock portfolio that carries less risk and a 100% bond portfolio that carries more risk. What matters more are the individual securities within the asset class. Here are some of the problems with the usual approach to asset allocation according to Cloonan:

- The correlation (movement together is "high" or apart is "low" correlation) between stocks and bonds changes all the time. Over the last 70 years the correlations have run from -0.3 to +0.6. How can you have an asset allocation plan that does not adjust for these differences?
- Diversifying between value and growth stocks is hard to do when, according to his estimation, only 15% of all stocks are true value and 15% are true growth. What do you call the rest of them?
- Most stock indexes will have over 20% of their assets invested in the largest 10 stocks; not only is this too much concentration, but the largest stocks often have high correlations.

Finally, if I have three clients, each with a 60/40 split between stocks and bonds, and I put one with the best performing managers, one with the worst-performing managers, and one in index funds, their returns will be vastly different, even though the asset allocation for each portfolio is the same. How can it be declared that asset allocation is responsible for 93.6% of a portfolio's return when three clients with the same allocation can have such widely varying results?[2]

Cynical view #2 – Can there be such a thing as over-diversification? Everyone knows the saying, "Don't put all your eggs in one basket," but no one asks the next question – "How many baskets should I have?" In his influential 1949 book *The Intelligent Investor,* legendary value investor Benjamin Graham argued that a portfolio of just 10 to 30 stocks provides adequate diversification. Increasing the number beyond that may reduce volatility marginally, but at the expense of higher transaction costs and more time required to monitor the portfolio.[3] Fortunately, a lot has happened in the investment world since 1949, in regards to investment fees, so it doesn't cost as much to diversify further. The question still remains, what is the optimal amount of diversification to reduce volatility, while not reducing returns? In his book, Common Stocks and Uncommon Profits, renowned investor, Philip Fisher, wrote an entire chapter on not overstressing diversification. In it he said, "This is the disadvantage of having eggs in so many baskets that a lot of the eggs do not end up in attractive baskets, and it is impossible to keep watching all the baskets after the eggs get put in them."[4] In a 1970, article by Lawrence Fisher and James H. Lorie, in *The Journal of Business*, entitled, "Some Studies of Variability of Returns on Investments in Common Stocks," they came to the conclusion that 32 stocks could reduce distribution by 95%, compared to a portfolio of the entire New York Stock Exchange.[5] From this came the mythical legend that "95% of the benefit of diversification is captured with a 30 stock portfolio."[5]

So Eric, what's the optimal number of stocks, mutual funds or Exchange Traded Funds (ETFs)? I won't give you a definitive number here, but I do have an approach to this question I will briefly discuss in the next chapter. Suffice it to say, I do believe that if you own every asset class then every year you will own the best returning asset classes and the worst performing assets classes and by definition will get the average of everything. My answer will hinge on the question, "Is it possible to avoid being in the worst performing asset classes?"

Cynical view #3 – You can't beat the Indexes, so why should I pay the extra fees for an active manager?

There is a lot packed into this question. Every year there are articles in popular financial magazines stating that 80% or more of active managers underperform their benchmarks. For me this is the wrong question. When it boils down to it, most investors want high returns with little to no risk. The problem is that this doesn't exist. The indexes themselves don't have expenses associated with them because they just report on what the various stocks associated with them return. Therefore, because index funds are managed by companies that have expenses, they will not match them exactly because of the internal expenses associated with them. But do you really want the returns of an index fund anyway?

I remember back in 2003, sitting down with a potential new client. We had discussed a number of financial planning issues, but when it got around to talking about investments his countenance took on a whole different look. I watched as his brow furrowed and arms crossed. "I invest in index funds," he smugly announced.

I nodded my head and replied, "So how did you like your returns last year?" I knew full well that the S&P 500 Index was down -22.1% in 2002.

"I didn't like it," he responded.

"Well, instead of staying 100% invested in stocks, which equity index funds do, active managers have the ability to intervene and move some money to cash, bonds, and other investments, which may help avoid losing as much."

Many times in new meetings I will ask the question a different way. "In 2008, the S&P 500 Index Fund was down -37%. I'm sure you wouldn't be happy with that, but would you be happy only being down -20%? Because there were mutual fund managers that were paid big bonuses for beating the index and only losing about half as much."

You would think that if someone wants to *beat the index*, they would be happy with only losing -20% instead of -37%, but I've never had someone respond that they were. What this really says to me, is that most investors are more interested in absolute returns versus relative returns.

Relative Returns are what your returns are in relation to whatever index you are measuring them against. For instance a large cap growth fund measured against the S&P 500 Index.

Absolute Returns are concerned with the return of a particular asset and how it fits in with the overall portfolio investment goal. So if someone comes to me with a desire to achieve a 5% annual return, then my goal is to design a portfolio of assets that will seek to hit that target year in and year out, regardless of what any of the Indexes are doing.

A prudent financial planning approach to investing is to review your long-term goals and determine what return is needed to accomplish them. Then you can make the best decision in regards to your investments. If you only need a 6% return, then you don't have to take higher risk to try and achieve 12% annual returns.

Cynical view #4 – Why can't I time the market to buy low and sell high?

"Timing is a wicked idea – don't try it, ever." Charles Ellis, author of, Investment Policy: How to Win the Loser's Game.

According to conventional wisdom, as the quote above purports, any attempt to time the market is fundamentally flawed. No one can predict the market's next move, so trying to do so will end up costing you money. A lot of your long-term gains will come from a few big "up" days, and these are completely unpredictable – if you are out of the market when they happen you will miss out on a lot of profits. Many financial advisors repeat this idea to clients. There is an industry bias for certain types of accounts, where advisors are not compensated for money market assets. If you are not invested then the advisor is not paid. Other accounts compensate an advisor regardless of the percentage of assets invested in stocks and bonds.

But is the idea correct?

The simple answer is, No... but.

Most people who try to time the market end up messing it up – they buy and sell at the wrong times – but that doesn't mean the idea is flawed.

Historically raising or lowering your exposure to either equities or fixed income assets, based on market fundamentals, has been one of the soundest ways to produce above-average investment returns over the long term. It is not about trying to trade short-term or market timing. It is not about selling stocks on Thursday and planning to buy them back the following Monday. It is about cutting your exposure to stocks when the market is expensive in relation to fundamentals, and keeping your exposure down – if need be, for years – until the market becomes much cheaper. It then involves increasing your exposure, and keeping it high, again for years if necessary.

Unfortunately, the emotions of fear and greed are typically what drive the stock market in the short run. Therefore as markets move up more and more, investors take more risk and some may even leverage their accounts through margin to seek even bigger gains. Then they ride it down, in a bear market and end up selling out of fear somewhere near the bottom.

If you don't have the time to understand fundamental investing and the ability to keep your emotions in check at extreme points in the market, then you are probably better off diversifying across at least four to five asset classes and investing on a monthly basis through dollar-cost averaging. Although in the next chapter I will discuss Momentum Investing and how it removes the desire to try and time the market.

CHAPTER 9

A BEACON OF LIGHT IN A STATUS QUO WORLD

Proactive investing in any market.

E conomic uncertainty is always present, but today's level of economic uncertainty is unlike anything most of us have experienced. Decades-long government deficit-spending policies, combined with actions aimed at diffusing the 2008 financial crisis, have created an investing climate which calls for fresh thinking about how to manage risk without giving up the opportunity for attractive returns.

Stocks, bonds, and gold have had major moves up in recent years, and to many investors, look overpriced. The million dollar question is this: *"Where does one invest in a world where everything looks expensive?"* There are certain foundational investment rules, such as – the older you get, the more your investments should shift away from stocks and towards bonds. This advice worked beautifully in recent decades as bond yields have fallen from the mid-teens to the low single-digits. As these yields have fallen, bond prices have risen, producing strong, stable returns year after year.

My concern recently has been that bonds will no longer provide the downside protection – the safe-haven aspect – that I have counted on to provide for clients. With bond prices at all-time highs as a result of the Federal Reserve pushing yields to unnatural lows, I feel it's safe to say the U.S. bond market has never been as overvalued as it is today.

Meanwhile, government borrowing has exploded. Like a rubber band wound tighter and tighter, a limit will eventually be reached. At some point, lenders will look at the massive debt loads that even "credit-worthy" borrowers such as the U.S. government are carrying and will demand higher returns (read higher interest rates) for the added risk. Bond yields will eventually rise, and bond prices will eventually fall. While higher rates will be welcomed by those on fixed income, it will bring a corresponding drop in principal. The only question is when.

Extreme Economic Uncertainty

Unfortunately, there's no such thing as a permanent safe haven in investing. This may come as a surprise to those who have watched money flood into U.S. Treasury bonds at every sign of trouble over the past decade. But we're reaching the point when government finances have become the *source* of the trouble. That point has arrived in Europe already, and may eventual come here as well.

Some feel the dominant financial issue of our time is how to deal with the massive amount of debt that governments around the world have amassed. The problem has been building for decades, but the tipping point was reached in the aftermath of 2008's financial crisis. The question is no longer *whether* something needs to be done, but how to deal *with it* and specifically *when*.

This "deleveraging" process – reducing debt in relation to income – can be attempted in different ways. One way is to cut spending, which is often referred to as "austerity." This has been the approach taken in Europe the past few years. What we've learned from watching their efforts is that austerity in the face of an already weak economy is extremely painful. This path caused dramatic recessions in much of Europe, creating a vicious cycle of lower income, leading to lower tax revenues, leading to even greater government debt. This process is deflationary by nature, meaning prices and wages fall as unemployment rises and demand for goods declines.

Not only does austerity cause great economic pain, it also gets democratically elected politicians voted out of office. This lesson hasn't been lost on politicians in other countries, as we've witnessed in recent U.S. elections and subsequent negotiations in regards to the fiscal cliff. Significant spending cuts, in today's environment, can be political suicide. Deflation and recession may well win out anyway, but the powers that be aren't going to surrender without fighting for more deficit spending. Europe eventually succumbed to this mindset and has embarked on their version of Quantitative Easing (QE).

An alternative approach to stimulating an economy has been what the central banks have been trying to do with their QE programs. QE is an unconventional monetary policy in which a central bank purchases government securities in order to lower interest rates and increase the money supply. To this point, these massive efforts have barely succeeded at keeping the global economy slightly above stall speed. The risk, of course, is that eventually inflation is ignited by these stimulative measures. It hasn't happened to this point because the deflationary impact of recessions and deleveraging has been overwhelming the otherwise inflationary policies. But this could change, perhaps without much warning, particularly if real economic growth did begin once again. Ironically, governments currently welcome modest inflation, as it helps them repay their debts in cheaper dollars. But this is a dangerous game, as inflation is not easily tamed once unleashed. Despite the obvious potential risks ahead, it's surprisingly easy to build an optimistic case, at least for the short term. The economy has muddled along, while the stock market has welcomed the easy money policy with significant increases since 2009. The problem is that there is no precedence for this type of action and it remains to be seen if this flood of money will cause much bigger problems in the future.

By some measures, the U.S. economy appears to be gaining strength. Corporations continue to see record earnings and are extremely well capitalized. And governments have shown an incredible ability to turn what seem to be crises into a long, protracted process instead. Even if a day of reckoning is coming, it still could be years away as politicians put duct-tape on the engine of the economy to try and keep it running. The Fiscal Cliff of 2012 is behind us, and while it ended up as a non-event, the minimal results have probably caused each political party to dig in deeper for the debate on raising the debt ceiling. Having witnessed several years in which by all rights the stock market should have dropped dramatically, but was rescued time and time again by the Fed's stimulative policies, I've determined once and for all that trying to predict the economic future is a losing game. But the stakes have rarely been higher, given the aforementioned valuation extremes in the bond market. *If bonds are no longer an adequate safe haven, where else can we turn?*

Finding Inspiration in the "Permanent Portfolio"

In the late 1970's, investment adviser Harry Browne began promoting an investing strategy he called the Permanent Portfolio (PP). The main idea behind it is that economic conditions change over time, cycling unpredictably through extremes of prosperity, inflation, recession, and deflation. Each of these phases produces specific investment winners and losers. What you want to own during a recession may well be the opposite of what will perform well during an economic recovery, and so on. Browne's solution was to divide a portfolio into four equal investments, each highly uncorrelated with the others (meaning the rise or fall of each does not depend on the other doing the same). One-fourth of the portfolio was to be allocated, respectively, to stocks, bonds, gold, and interest-earning short-term investments such as U.S. Treasury bills (referred to as "cash" for short). These were selected because each would excel under a different economic extreme. Thus, the portfolio would always have at least one of the four pieces completely in tune with the current environment. Other than rebalancing periodically, this mix was unchanging, thus the Permanent Portfolio name.

This exceedingly simple approach has performed quite admirably over the last 15 years. From 2000 – 2014, such a portfolio gained 125.09% or roughly 8.34% per year. The S&P 500 gained only 42.83% over that same 15 years, or 2.85% per year. However, like in most things, statistics can tell a different story over a different period of analysis. If we measure the longer 33 year period from 1982 through the end of 2014, then we find that the Permanent Portfolio averaged 7.61% as compared to the S&P 500 Index's 11.03%.[1] Of course the 7.61% came with significantly less volatility and risk. Remember, only 25% of the Permanent Portfolio was in stocks. The real virtue of this approach was how little volatility it generated: in 2008 the return was -8.36% versus the S&P 500 Index being down -37%. And, in 2000, 2001 and 2002, when the S&P 500 Index was down -9.1%, -11.9% and -22.1%, respectively, the Permanent Portfolio was up 5.88%, 3.81% and 14.36%.[1]

While there are many things to like about the PP strategy, there are two significant downsides. First, while it achieves my goal with clients of reducing risk, this system may be more conservative than many investors need. Allocating one-fourth of one's' portfolio to cash may have made sense in the late 1970s when that would earn 15% in a money-market fund. Today, cash earns virtually nothing, so permanently fixing a quarter of the portfolio there may not be practical. To help counter this, there is a need to expand the basket of asset classes beyond the four proposed by Harry Browne.

The second problem has less to do with the portfolio and more to do with human nature. The PP has looked great over the past decade or so, due to stocks being weak while bonds and gold have been soaring. It will normally look its best following sharp bear markets in stocks, of which we've had two in the past dozen years. But there have been long stretches when the PP lagged the market badly. Many investors lack the willpower to stick with an approach like this when stocks are soaring in comparison.

Stocks gained more than 20% for five straight years from 1995-1999, while the PP earned more than 11% only once. Investors simply don't stick with systems at times like those – the emotional component, (of missing out on better returns, known as regret) is simply too powerful. And yet, the years that followed were exactly the time to embrace the Permanent Portfolio. Unfortunately, the idea of a static portfolio with no "switching mechanism" would have likely led many to miss the gains of 1995-1999, only to switch to stocks in time to experience the sharp losses of 2000-2002. That said, *"Is there a momentum mechanism that makes sense?"*

The Breakthrough: Adding a Momentum Element

While a pure application of PP has the issues noted above, it does elevate the importance of using non-correlated asset classes in an attempt to achieve higher returns with lower risk. The following study was performed by the analysts at Sound Mind Investing (SMI), as noted here: "The breakthrough came when we started testing what happens when we own *only the asset classes showing momentum at that particular time* rather than owning all of them *all* the time." By "momentum," they mean owning three of six asset classes that have the strongest relative strength of the six and monitoring monthly to see if changes need to be made due to a change in momentum (or return). SMI continued, "After much testing and numerous iterations, we emerged with a simple but powerful strategy. Our roster of asset classes eventually expanded to six: the PP's original four, plus foreign and real estate stocks. (They call it Dynamic Asset Allocation or DAA).

Using these six asset classes, we applied a momentum screen at the beginning of each month, identifying the three asset classes we wanted to be in and – perhaps more importantly – the three we wanted to avoid. Each month we re-ran the screen and adjusted our holdings as required. The results were very impressive."[2]

Exchange Traded Funds (ETFs) are one of the least expensive and purest ways to own an asset class; therefore, the following ETFs represent each of the six asset classes:

> U.S. Stocks – *SPDR S&P 500 ETF®* (**SPY**)
> Foreign Stocks – *iShares MSCI EAFE®* (**EFA**)
> Gold – *SPDR Gold Trust®* (**GLD**)
> Real Estate – *Vanguard REIT ETF®* (**VNQ**)
> Bonds – *Vanguard L-T Bond®* (**BLV**)
> Cash – *iShares Barclays TB®* (**SHY**)

The key to DAA's success and what I like is 'winning by not losing.' By dramatically reducing losses, this strategy is able to come out ahead in the long run, even though it doesn't earn as much when stocks are soaring. Most importantly, this is a strategy that risk-averse investors can stick with. That's crucial, as even the most profitable systems are worthless if investors can't handle the volatility they experience along the way and end up selling everything out of fear.

Winning by Not Losing

Remember, the beginning point of this journey was to find a replacement for bonds as a safe haven for risk-averse investors. If boosting a portfolio's bond allocation wasn't going to provide the safety from future market storms that we've counted on in the past, we needed something else that would. That's the real value of this new strategy.

In comparing the returns of DAA vs. the S&P 500 over a 33 year period, a few things stood out. First, DAA has only had one losing year, a loss of -6.6% in 1990. While in the years 2000-2002 and 2008, the strategy outperformed. During this time, stocks were plummeting and investors were full of panic and fear, the DAA strategy was up +7.1%, +4.0%, +10.4% and +1.3%, respectively.[3] As always in looking at investment returns in hindsight, it's important to understand that this is not a guarantee that there will not be losing years going forward. This is merely the picture of what has happened in the past.

The DAA strategy outperformed the stock market while being less volatile. This shows that indeed, slow and steady can win the race.

Adding Responsible Alpha

In investing, Alpha is defined as a measure of performance on a risk-adjusted basis. If a mutual fund has a positive Alpha, that means that in comparison to its benchmark index, the fund had a better return. The manager has "added Alpha" or additional returns in relation to the risk taken. A way that I seek to add Alpha to client portfolios is by utilizing the same relative strength analysis done in the DAA strategy with Sector and Country funds.

In his 2006 book, "ETF Trading Strategies Revealed," David Vomund, does extensive research on the use of momentum, through the calculation of Relative Strength. The historical evidence he presents for using this analysis with sector and country funds is very compelling.[4]

Sector ETFs are typically diversified in their number of holdings, but concentrate on stocks within the same category. For example, a Utilities Sector ETF might hold Duke Energy, Southern Company, Pacific Gas & Electric and fifty other utility stocks. Each month I analyze approximately 40 different sectors (such as Energy Biotechnology, Utilities, Telecommunications, Aerospace, Semiconductors, Retail, Health Care, Transportation), and invest in the top two performing funds, as determined by their relative strength numbers. At the end of the next month I will analyze the same 40 sectors. If one or both of the funds fall out of the top 25% (out of the top 10), then I sell one or both of them and rotate into the new top one or two.

In the same way, **Country ETFs** are diversified in their number of holdings, but concentrate on stocks within the same country. In the United States we are familiar with the S&P 500 Index, which is comprised of the 500 largest stocks on the New York Stock Exchange. Most countries have their version of the S&P 500 Index, which is comprised of the largest stocks on their respective exchanges. Each month I analyze approximately 40 different countries (such as Japan, Brazil, Italy, Belgium, New Zealand, Canada, Malaysia, etc.), and invest in the two top performing country funds. I then follow the same procedure as the sector funds with monthly analysis and replacement if necessary.

Since sector and country funds tend to have greater volatility, I will typically put in limit orders or trailing stops to help protect a client's downside risk. By putting in a limit order, I can set a price to sell an ETF at a specific price or better. This can be useful after a rise in the share price to sell at a price above where we purchased the shares and capture a gain. The other option is to put in a trailing stop. In doing this I can determine a percentage, for example 10%, that I can set for an ETF. If the ETF rises 10%, for example from $100 a share to $110 a share, then the stop order to sell will rise from $90 to $100. In a rising market these orders can be useful to follow the share price up and then sell to capture gains if there is a reversal in the share price.

Again, while not guaranteeing positive returns, the strategy of proactively moving out of sector and country funds whose relative strength is declining and into those that are rising, is a potential way to add alpha to a portfolio. *Another advantage of this strategy is that it is driven by math and not my personal opinion.* The numbers tell me to move into say, the Transportation Fund and Italy Fund, not the fact that I like a new car I just bought and returned from a fabulous trip to the lush countryside in Tuscany. In a very real sense this turns the concern over *'the markets are rising so much, where do I invest?'* into a positive versus a negative.

Tactical Asset Rotation Strategy (TARS)

One thing I like about finances and investing is that everything has an acronym, much like the military. Some of these would include:

SEALs – Sea, Air, Land
BUPERs - BUreau of naval PERSonnel
CIC – Combat Information Center
CO – Commanding Officer
DoD – Department of Defense
EAOS – End of Active Obligated Service
EOD – Explosive Ordnance Disposal
FOD – Foreign Object Damage (Essential debris)
FTN – Forget The Navy (Polite Form)
GQ – General Quarters (Not the magazine, this is a call to battle stations)
NCIS – Naval Criminal Investigative Service
PAX – Passengers
POD – Plan Of the Day
POTUS – President Of The United States
RIO – Radar Intercept Officer (Think Goose backing up Maverick in the movie Top Gun)
WTF – Whiskey Tango Foxtrot (Usually an interrogative phrase, but may also be used in a declarative manner)
XO – Executive Officer (Second in Command)

So of course, I couldn't help myself and developed TARS to describe my variation on the momentum strategy using relative strength numbers. Unlike Sound Mind Investing's DAA strategy, which only uses 3, 6 and 12 month returns for its analysis, I add 1 month returns as well. In addition, unlike David Vomund, when it comes to sector and country investing, I incorporate trailing stops to try and mitigate downside losses between monthly reviews.

Passive Versus Active Investing Debate
Passive management

Passive investing, commonly referred to as "indexing," is a natural outgrowth of the Efficient Market Hypothesis (EMH), which argues that because of the collective efforts of the market's millions of participants, all of the known information about a given security is *already reflected* in its price. Therefore, stock prices should be regarded as an accurate estimate of the investment's intrinsic value, such that it's pointless to try to find undervalued stocks with the expectation of outperforming the overall market.

If an investor's starting point is "it's impossible to beat the market," then the most sensible approach is to simply build a portfolio that essentially replicates the market, while paying the lowest possible fees to do so. In this view, there's no point in taking active measures trying to beat a market that can't be beaten, so a passive approach makes the most sense.

Active management

Active managers believe that the market isn't perfectly efficient, which leaves open the possibility of improving on the market's overall result. The most common goal of active management is to earn returns that are better than a benchmark that represents a particular investment (the S&P 500, for example, often is used as a benchmark for "beating the market").

In some cases, other goals are pursued by active managers. For example, an investment might attempt to earn the *same return* as the market, but with *less volatility*. Whatever the specific goal, the premise is that taking certain actions can provide a benefit compared to passive investing.

Passive vs active: Who wins?

The debate over whether passive investing is fundamentally superior to active attempts to beat the market has become an ideological struggle for superiority, with big money riding on the outcome. Accordingly, a huge amount of academic research has been done on the passive vs. active subject. The vast majority of it finds in favor of passive investing. However, even with passive investing, the returns are going to be reduced by the expenses of the passive index funds (despite them being very low) That leaves investors with returns that equal the index invested in less the total expenses extracted. On average, then, investors' returns are going to trail the index's return due to these expenses.

Much of the research on passive vs. active investing focuses on the cumulative analysis. Looking at *all* the mutual funds in existence over an extended time period, will invariably show that, in total, they lagged the market. It would be impossible for them not to. You are lumping together all the good, active managers, with the bad.

The relevant question for investors isn't whether actively managed funds can outperform the market *as a group*. The answer to that is always going to be no. Rather, the real question is whether there's a realistic way to identify *specific individual* active investment strategies that will outperform the market. That's a very different issue than grouping all active investment attempts together.

Enter Momentum "BIG MO"

My **Tactical Asset Rotation Strategy (TARS)** is based on the investment principle of **momentum**. The definition of momentum as it relates to investing is simply *the tendency of investment performance to persist.* Investments that have done well will continue to do well, while those that have done poorly will continue to do poorly. [5]

Most investors are unaware that performance momentum has a long history of academic support. The earliest scientific study and published academic paper in support of momentum dates back over 90 years to 1924, and there have been many since, including a flurry of research done in recent decades. [6]

One reason performance momentum has been so heavily studied in recent years is that it has been a persistent thorn in the side of the efficient-markets crowd. Remember, the EMH believes that a phenomenon like investing momentum should not exist. So when faced with a seeming contradiction to their theory, believers in the EMH have a strong incentive to explain away such anomalies. Yet in the case of momentum, no less an authority than Eugene Fama, often referred to as the father of the EMH, called momentum "the center stage anomaly of recent years... the premier anomaly is momentum."

It is important to qualify that the academic research is quite clear that momentum is a relatively short-term phenomenon. The research demonstrates that performance persists over periods of 12 months or less. This is why the old advice regarding how to select mutual funds is worthless: identifying funds with good long-term (3, 5, or 10-year) track records has no bearing on which funds are likely to perform well over the coming year. *Longer*-term performance simply is not predictive. But *short*-term performance has repeatedly been shown to be predictive. Again, these are not my claims, this is what numerous academic studies have concluded. One of the best books on the topic with references is, *"Momentum Due Diligence"* by Gary Autonacci, June 18, 2015. [7]

Recognizing that momentum is one of the few *proven* anomalies to the EMH, but that momentum is inherently a short-term phenomenon, requires me to continually monitor client investments for changes in momentum. Unlike indexers, I don't have the luxury of buying a particular set of investments and holding them forever. The price of trying to outperform the market (and minimize the damage done by bear markets such as investors experienced in 2008) is that I have to stay engaged with our investments. This is why the TARS strategies include monthly "check-ups" where I determine if changes are needed.

Passive, Active — or something better?

Using momentum to select investments in an effort to beat the market is inherently an active-management approach. But it can be employed utilizing passive investment vehicles.

For example, in the Tactical Asset Rotation Strategy (TARS), I monitor and compare broad asset classes—U.S. stocks vs. bonds vs. real estate vs. gold, etc. The most efficient and least expensive way to get exposure to these broad asset classes is to use Index Exchange Traded Funds (ETFs), which are passively managed vehicles.

So in TARS, I am using an *active* management technique to select *passive* investments. This same momentum strategy is also utilized with Sectors and Countries, as I discussed previously.

Over the long-term, these active strategies have provided returns well in excess of what the market has provided. In recent years, specifically since the 2008 financial crisis, indexing has had the upper hand over most active strategies. It's not unusual for index funds to outperform during bull markets such as we've had in recent years, but that script often changes during bear markets. That is why the "active" side of this strategy is employed to move out of "bull market" style ETFs (primarily stocks) when the markets are going up, and into more "bear market" style ETFs (like Bonds, Gold and Treasuries), when the markets are going down.

CHAPTER 10

THE THREE C'S

Contentment, College and Coffee.

Contentment - The Merriam-Webster dictionary defines contentment as, "a state of happiness and satisfaction." With all due respect to Merriam, I believe the Bible provides us with a much fuller description of what it means to be content. Philippians 4:11 says, "I have learned to be content whatever the circumstances," and 1 Timothy 6:6 says, "Godliness with contentment is great gain."

The world is a crazy place, in many ways. Society values certain vocations more than others through the reward of money. Professional athletes make more in a few years than our school teachers will make in a lifetime. When I discussed careers with my children, I would tell them they can be anything they want to be. It doesn't matter to me (or God for that matter). But when it comes to earning a living, you have to be prepared to be content with the value society places on your chosen vocation. Being content is the ability to remain satisfied with one's standard of living, whether high or low.

In 1987 I was a First Class Midshipman (Senior) at the Naval Academy. Those of us majoring in Economics went on the annual trip to Wall Street. The United States was in the midst of a huge economic boon under President Reagan, patriotism was high and I was being wined and dined at the Wall Street Club, on the top of a skyscraper in New York City. Upon our return a few of us went to see the new Oliver Stone movie, "Wall Street." You may recall the villain of the film, Gordon Gekko, played by Michael Douglas. His most famous line was, "Greed, for lack of a better word, is good." Unfortunately many people bought into that line and while the short-term consequences might be higher productivity, a sense of accomplishment, and economic growth, the long-term consequences are anything but. The reality is that your life can't be balanced if you constantly desire something you don't have. Greed generally grows out of the impulse to "keep up with the Joneses." It is the temptation to evaluate your lifestyle by comparing it with that of other people. How do you know if you're giving into this temptation? Do a self-evaluation. When you're driving into work or around town are your thoughts on your spouse, children, and the next social event with other people or is it on the new luxury car that just passed by or the bigger house you want so badly?

Greed can come into play on the job as well. In certain careers this is more evident than others. But, it always seems to come out when money is on the line. In the financial services industry everything centers on money. I remember pre-2008, there were lavish incentive trips. They were designed to motivate advisors to increase the size and revenue of their book of business. It didn't change *my* behavior. I figured if I did what was right for the client my business would grow and if I happened to fall into the category for a trip then I went. Even though the company didn't pay for children, I always used the trips as a time for family and paid to bring them along.

With my military and sports background, I've always been a team player. It's interesting to observe different advisors responses to situations when fees or commissions are on the line. Technically, everyone has their own business and in that regard advisors are all competitors, even when we work for the same firm on the same floor. But there are opportunities to do joint work. When one advisor has a client who has a problem and another advisor knows the solution, they can work together and split the fee or commission anyway they decide. The phrase we used to identify this was, "50% of something is better than 100% of nothing." The meaning being, it's better to get a case completed and be paid half the fee than to not do the case at all. Typically one advisor would have the intellectual capital and ensure things got done correctly for the other advisor's client. Over the course of the analysis and application, the assisting advisor was learning, so that in the future he could do it on his own. A win-win for both parties involved. Unfortunately I've also been around advisors where I had the intellectual capital and they used that to get their case done and then didn't follow through financially for my efforts. The phrase for that is, "pigs get fat and hogs get slaughtered." In the short-run there may be a financial advantage for taking short cuts or not treating people fairly, but in the long-run others get to know that person for who they really are and don't want to have much to do with them.

A positive story from the past (at least the two of us get a laugh out of it), was when I asked another advisor to help me with a client for an issue that was outside my area of expertise. It wasn't going to result in a lot of fees, but the client was a professional athlete and I think the advisor wanted to meet him. We drove over an hour to get to the appointment and after spending some time to get all the information we needed, we left and began working on the case. The bottom line is that after spending a lot of time on it and presenting our findings, the client didn't move forward. We were paid nothing for our efforts. I coined a new phrase that day. "50% of nothing is better than 100% of nothing." Meaning, it's more fun to have two people get nothing than to get nothing on your own. Years later we still laugh about that.

College – A few thoughts on college planning. First and foremost I want to relieve any guilt parents may be feeling by verifying for you that there is nothing in the Bible or the United States Constitution that says you have to pay for your child's college tuition. In planning with clients, it sometimes feels like they put paying for college ahead of their own retirement. I have one college graduate, one child graduating from college and headed off to graduate school and my youngest is a new college student. From my experience of saving, incentivizing and spending on college, I don't think there is much I would change. So here are my top 10 suggestions:

1. Put some money away monthly the day your kids are born. $100 a month into a growth stock mutual fund or a college 529 plan can make a big difference over eighteen years. Investing $100 a month, with a hypothetical average return of 8%, would be worth $48,535, at the end of 18 years.

2. Provide incentives. I let my kids know in middle school that if they got a full ride to college I'd buy them a new car. It should be obvious from that statement that I don't recommend buying your child a new car on their 16th birthday. One of my three actually achieved this goal. You can also put smaller incentives in place for grades and other college-resume building items that might lead to scholarship money.

3. Have a college reality check. I know some parents who have told their children, "Whatever University you get into, I'll figure out a way to pay for it." In my opinion, which is also backed up by a number of studies, unless you get into one of the top ten elite universities in the country, your future income potential is driven much more by the student than the school. Public universities charge a huge premium to out of state students. If you live in Florida, your tuition will be more than five times as high to go to the University of South Carolina versus Florida State University. In 2015-2016 school year, the in-state tuition as FSU was $5,644[1] and out-of-state tuition at USC was $29,440[2]. With all due respect to both universities, in my opinion, there isn't a $95,184 difference for that four year degree.

4. Have a time budget. It was clearly understood in my house that college was a 4-year endeavor. According to the National Student Clearinghouse, a nonprofit verification and research organization, only 66% of students earned their degree within six years.[3] Granted, it was mandatory to graduate in 4-years at the Naval Academy, but I was also taking 18-21 credit hours a semester (needless to say, sympathy for my kid's anguish over a 15 credit hour semester wasn't very high). My wife graduated from a civilian school in 4 years as well. I wanted it to be very clear. Mom and Dad aren't paying for you to extend your social life and avoid the real world. You can take longer than 4 years, but our financial contribution ends there. One of my daughters asked, "If I finish my degree in 3-1/2 years, will you pay for half a year of my Master's degree?" We were more than happy to do this. It showed a great deal of forethought and effort on her part to do this.

5. Have a total tuition budget. If you haven't heard of the Benjamin Franklin method of making a decision, it's when you list the pros and cons of each option you have on paper, then compare them. This is a great exercise to help your up and coming college student visualize their options. My oldest daughter was a classic example. There was an out-of-state private college, an in-state public university and an in-state private college. On a spreadsheet or paper, list each school at the top and along the side list all the factors you are comparing. The first should be the tuition, room & board, and other expenses. I then reduced those by the scholarships she received from the schools, independent sources and Florida Bright Futures (our state's contribution for good students staying in-state). I also netted out money we had set aside in 529 plans, Uniform Trust to Minor Accounts (UTMAs) and State Pre-paid plans. Lastly, my wife and I had sent our children to a private high school, so we said we would continue with this expense for their 4-years. Subtracting all of these contributions to tuition resulted in the bottom-line net expense for each college option. I explained that this was the amount she was going to be responsible for. *But dad, all of my friend's parents said they would pay whatever the cost is to go to college.* "That may be true, honey, but I'm not your friend's parents." The result was that in the case of the in-state public university, her expense would be $0. The out-of-state private college offered the most scholarship money, but it was going to cost her $2,500 a year. There were a lot of other factors, including; class size, city versus rural, extra-curricular opportunities, total student enrollment, etc.), but the net cost to my kids suddenly became an issue they would have to wrestle with. They now had to question whether the value of the private university or out-of-state college was worth paying for. They were going to have skin in the game.

6. *Have a school year budget.* Setting up a bank account with ATM access at the college and depositing a nominal amount each semester is a great way to teach budgeting. It can be a few hundred dollars, but it provides your son or daughter with the opportunity to make decisions on going out for pizza, getting their daily coffee, or a school spirit tee shirt. If the money runs out quickly then their options become limited and a behavioral change takes place the next semester. I've actually enjoyed conversations where my daughter's would approach me for a semester allowance increase. I'd have them put a budget on paper and present

their case. Feel free to present this chapter to your rising college student and play good-cop, bad-cop. *Aren't you glad Mr. Reinhold isn't your father?*

7. The college car discussion. Every family has to address the car decision for their high school student and then college student. You already know my thoughts on a new car for a 16 year old. We actually traded in an old van, during the "Cash for Clunkers" deal President Obama rolled out early in his administration, and bought a Hyundai Elantra, with a 10-year, 100,000 mile warranty to be passed along among our three children over a 10-year span in high school.

I remember when my daughter was a senior in high school and came back from an out-of-state college visit. She was excited to tell me all the details. She had memorized a lot of statistics while on her visit and during our conversation she slipped this comment in:

"Dad, 96% of the students have a car at XYZ College."

I thought about it for a second and replied, "Great, then you won't have a problem getting around."

I'm pretty sure that wasn't the response she was looking for.

Our personal conviction was that our kids would be better served without a car their first few years in college. I'm proud to say that my oldest daughter decided to go to the private out-of-state college, worked and paid for the uncovered tuition portion, and then transferred to an in-state public university after two years. By graduation she had no student debt, purchased a nice, used car in cash, fully funded a ROTH IRA and still had money in the bank. My second daughter is working to pay the, uncovered portion of the in-state, private university she is attending and as I mentioned, will finish in 3-1/2 years. The money she is saving by finishing early will help pay for her Master's degree.

8. School books. One of the most outrageous expenses of a college education is the cost of books. College textbook prices are 812 percent higher than they were a little more than three decades ago, according to a think tank called the American Enterprise Institute.[4] Textbook costs have outpaced the 559 percent increase in tuition and fees over roughly the same period. With college bookstores receiving just over 20% of the sales price, there is an incentive for the University to keep sales in house.[5] In addition, over the past decade, there has been a battle back and forth between textbook publishers and the consumer. The first competitor was the off-campus used bookstore. Colleges countered with buy-backs and used book sales of their own, but then upped the ante with professors getting paid to publish new editions, with only minor changes, and then requiring the new versions. In the past few years, a new on-line industry has emerged, selling new and used books, as well as renting them. Publishers have tried to counter this by packaging books with bundled software or on-line codes which will only work once, and making certain editions university specific to reduce competition. Unfortunately the adverse effect has been for students to forgo the books altogether, relying on making copies of certain sections from other student's books or just taking notes in class.

The most cost effective method I have found to procure textbooks is to rent them on-line. It removes the hassle of buying and selling new or used books and typically costs less than the net of those transactions as well. Most on-line businesses provide free labels for shipping the books back at the end of the semester.

One of my daughters received an update from her college that they were moving to a new system that "re-bundles" tuition with books. This program is called *IncludED*. The school sent out a notice stating this program, "allows schools to provide required course materials to students as part of tuition or fees, ensuring students understand the full cost of education upfront and are prepared with required course materials on day one." They are mandating participation for general education courses. The fees for the 20015-2016 school year would be $80 per book. Maybe it's just the cynic in me, but could this possibly be collusion between dinosaur textbook publishers who don't want internet competition and the college that gets a 20% take of the sale? I don't think I've ever had to pay $80 to rent a textbook for the semester. Fortunately my daughter has finished general education classes, so I might miss out on this *new, good deal* (sarcasm intended).

9. To work or not to work while in college? My views on this question have evolved over the past few years. While my children were in high school I was of the opinion that they should limit working to the summer and use their free-time during the school year for sports, extracurricular activities, and social interaction with friends.

While I still maintain that view for high school, my views on working during college have changed. Both of my daughters have worked during college and it has been a positive experience for them. It has allowed them to stay debt-free, given them some extra spending money, and also provided invaluable experience in working with others. Even though my oldest daughter is interviewing in a completely different career field than the sector she worked in during college, interviewers have commented favorably on a number of factors that go with working during college. These characteristics include, timeliness, balancing a schedule, interaction with customers, and a strong work ethic.

10. Don't leave money on the table. Scholarships given by colleges are the most common type and are typically automatic, based upon grades, SAT/ACT scores, athletics, music or other extracurricular activities. There are also national scholarships from large corporations, which you can research on the internet, but the best places to search first are local scholarships sponsored by, your church or religious denomination, Rotary Club, Kiwanis, American Legion, your employer, and local businesses. One of the best ways to fund college, which I participated in, is through a military service academy or ROTC program. Both of the processes are very time consuming and you need to be looking into it no later than Spring of your student's Junior year in high school.[6] Yes, there is a five year military commitment after graduation, but I also looked at it as guaranteed job placement. In addition, after five years you can choose to continue a military career or you can apply for a job with real world experience, discipline and management skills that all employers covet. Through the Service Academies, tuition, room and board, and books are 100% paid for, while ROTC covers everything but room and board. In addition, you are paid while you're going to school. Not all colleges have an ROTC program. Of those that do, many only have one branch of the service offered. If your son or daughter is interested, my suggestion is to first investigate what branch of the service would be the best fit. Next pursue the Service Academy associated with that branch and conduct an internet search to see what colleges have ROTC programs for that branch of the service. My son is interested in the Navy, so he applied to the Naval Academy, but we also researched what colleges in the South have a Navy ROTC programs and visited them over the spring break of his junior year. On his application for a Navy ROTC scholarship he can now confidently list his top 5 colleges.

Coffee – *a drink made from the roasted and ground beanlike seeds of a tropical shrub, served hot or cold.*

Life's too short to drink cheap coffee... I think you can tell a lot about a person by the coffee they drink. I don't think of myself as a coffee snob, but if you tell me your favorite coffee is from the most famous chain in the world, then I'll do my best not to burst out laughing. They've mastered, marketing the coffee experience, despite using the worst grade beans in the industry and burning them in the roasting process to boot. Actually the first time I had a cup of coffee from this chain, I had flashbacks to my days onboard the USS Yosemite (AD-19). I would stop by the wardroom to get some coffee before the mid-watch (that's standing duty on the bridge of the ship from 0330 – 0730 in the morning). The only coffee available had been cooking on the burner for about 12 hours. It smelled like burnt toast. Physically it resembled more of a food group than a liquid. It wasn't the caffeine that woke you up, it was the effort to try and choke it down.

What makes a good cup of coffee? To begin with, you should be able to drink it black. If you have to add spoonful's of sugar, flood it with dairy products, whip cream, syrups, or artificial sweeteners, then you aren't drinking real coffee (or you're ordering at Charbucks). *The fresher the coffee the better the taste.* At the very least that means grinding your beans. I enjoy buying green coffee beans (yes, they are green before you roast them) and then putting them in my roaster. I can close my eyes, while the machine hums, breath in the aroma, and imagine I'm at my favorite coffee roasters on the north shores of Oahu, Hawaii.

If you're not a coffee drinker, then fill in this blank – Life's too short to _____.

While the *one thing* is spending less than you earn over a long period of time and a big part of that is keeping a budget, there are some things worth splurging on. The key is using moderation and determining what those things are. It will differ for each individual and if you're married, then this is one of those discussions worth having together... over a cup of coffee.

Here are some of my "life's too short" items:

- When I'm on vacation and debating whether to purchase a moderately priced item that will remind me of the trip. I've determined that it's probably worth spending on, since I may never return in my lifetime. It was the case with my honeymoon, where we visited a quaint town in Southwest England, which we wanted to remember and have never returned.
- Again on vacations, I pick and choose where I'll cut costs and where I'll splurge. I've found $12 a day rental cars on Priceline, love discount airlines like Southwest (especially not paying baggage fees), but will upgrade my hotel because a hotel can make or break the vacation experience for me.
- A comfortable bed can be a *life's too short* item. Yes, try to find a good deal, but you're spending approximately 2,000 hours a year in it, so don't sacrifice comfort for price.

Time with family is another priority for me. It was amazing how quickly my children aged from the terrible two's to graduating from high school. I'll never regret putting them to bed at night, family vacations, sporting events, camping, and talks wherever and whenever. In fact when our children turned sixteen I took them on a trip wherever they wanted to go (Within reason, we couldn't go to a foreign country where my wife had never travelled). With one daughter we went to New York City, shopped and took in several musicals. My other daughter wanted to go on a Caribbean cruise. My son and I travelled to the Florida Keys to fish and snorkel. When we returned, we created a picture book through Shutterfly.com to capture the highlights and relive the memories.

There is a difference between *living for the moment* and *life's too short* moments. To me, living for the moment is to ignore the future and in a sense, spend like there's no tomorrow. *Life's too short* moments bring a balance to being so focused on tomorrow that you don't leave time to focus on the important issues of today. This is another great topic of communication between you and your spouse.

CHAPTER 11

ARE YOU SQUINTING IN A FOG OR IS THE SUN SHINING BRIGHT?

What will retirement look like for me?

*W*e *don't yet see things clearly. We're squinting in a fog, peering through a mist. But it won't be long before the weather clears and the sun shines bright! We'll see it all then, see it all as clearly as God sees us, knowing him directly just as he knows us! I Corinthians 13:12* (The Message)

While the above scripture verse is referencing how we see God while on earth versus when we meet him in heaven, I believe there is application for how we see our retirement now and what we will see when that day arrives.

Where the bucket list and reality meet.

If you proactively choose not to live life on a budget or by default just ignore making a budget and live for the moment, then *you* will hurt your retirement income. Retirement is a balancing act. You want to spend enough to enjoy today (which we discussed in the previous chapter), while preserving enough to take care of your essentials and lifestyle desires tomorrow.

What are some specific issues which throw people off balance on their journey to retirement? Here are five things people do that put them at risk for running out of money.

1. No measurement gauge. When I bought a 10-year old, used truck, to haul things around and let my son drive his senior year in high school, several items were in need of repair. On the instrument panel both the speedometer and fuel gauge didn't work. Imagine driving around town with no fuel tank gauge. How often do you stop for gas? You would have to guess.

It would be the same case with the speedometer. It's possible that you could drive the same speed of those around you, but what if they're driving over the speed limit? When the police officer stopped you and asked, "Do you know how fast you were going?" I don't think, "No officer I don't, my speedometer doesn't work," would be a good response.

If you approach retirement income this way, you can get yourself in trouble. You must have a monitoring system in place. This type of system measures how much you have left, your income needs, uses a conservative rate of return based on your investing style, and takes into account remaining life expectancy. Your retirement income instrument panel isn't only there to tell you when to slow down – it can also tell you when there is room to step on the gas.

2. No spending plan. In keeping with the theme of this book, spending more than you have in retirement will certainly cause you to run out of money. Most often excess spending occurs as parents help adult children, or because an upcoming retiree forgot to calculate expected taxes and health care expenses into their retirement budget.

Before you retire, you should have your house paid off and all major expenses you can foresee taken care of. This would be items like remodeling the house, putting a new roof on, or purchasing a new car. The lower your monthly expenses can be the better. A monthly mortgage is typically one of the biggest line items people have in their budget, so having your house paid off before you retire will really put your mind at ease. In addition, you don't want to have big purchases in the first few years of retirement, while you adjust to your new lifestyle. Your psyche will take a hit if you see your savings depleted by spending a big chunk of money on a new roof, boat or car, six months into retirement.

When you retire, make a spending plan that lays out your monthly and annual expenditures, including money for fun. Now, add up your guaranteed sources of income, like Social Security or a pension. The amount of living expenses in excess of your guaranteed income must come from your savings and investments.

Make a projection assuming you take the desired withdrawals, and see how long the money lasts. Now, make the same projection, but assume you spend $5,000 more or less a year. This type of scenario modeling is what I do to show clients how small changes in their spending can make the difference between having enough money or running out.

3. Invest wrong. Your investment goal in retirement is not to maximize returns, nor, contrary to what many believe, is it to preserve principal. What most retirees want is sustainable lifelong income. This is not the time to go for the hot stock tip, nor is it the time to keep all your money in certificates of deposit while inflation whittles away at your purchasing power.

This is the time to learn about the various investment philosophies for retirement income, and decide on the one most appropriate for you. Here are four approaches to consider:

- *The income-only approach*: You only spend the interest and dividends that your investments generate.
- *The systematic withdrawal approach*: You build a risk/return adjusted portfolio with a target annualized rate of return of about 6 to 7 percent and you plan on taking withdrawals of about 4 percent a year.
- *The time segmentation approach*: You match investments to upcoming cash flow needs, so your safe investments are used for spending in the first 10 years of retirement, and your growth investments can be left alone to accumulate for years 11 and beyond.
- *The guaranteed income approach*: You use annuity products to guarantee a lifelong income.

The secret to retirement investing success is to pick an approach and stick with it. Jumping from one investment approach to another is bound to set you back and create frustration.

4. No plan B. Life throws curveballs, not only while you are saving for retirement, but while you are in it as well. If your plan requires you to use every asset you have, you're at risk of running out of money. You need to allocate some of your assets to cash reserves. This means that these assets are not included in your plan as available to meet living expenses in retirement.

Reserves can be an emergency fund account, home equity, cash in the safe, a vacation house, or even a valued collectible. If it is a non-liquid asset, it should be one that you can convert to cash in a short period of time. Hopefully you'll never need to tap into your reserves, but it may be you'll need it for health care expenses later in life, or to help an adult child who gets in trouble. There's no telling what might come up that throws your original plan off track. That's why you need assets set aside as plan B.

5. Fall for the scam. There will never be a shortage of people trying to part you from your money. In our own family, my wife's grandmother had a financial advisor who listed a number of financial assets on the net worth statement he provided her that weren't there. It was sad to have to report this to others in the family when I made the discovery.

There are countless stories in the news, of not just retirees, but professional athletes and others falling for scams that promised them outstanding returns. As you age, your ability to process complex financial decisions declines. Unfortunately, you maintain a strong belief that you have the capacity to process such things the same way you always have. This is not a good combination.

"Plans fail for lack of counsel, but with many advisers they succeed." Proverbs 15:22

Whether it is a family member or professional, it is wise to have a trusted advisor who you can turn to before making money decisions. Ironically, some people wait until they are in their 50s or 60s to establish this relationship, when they feel they have enough money. But my experience has shown me that it's better to seek out a financial advisor sooner rather than later. Why? I've started working with older clients who I wish I had met sooner so that they hadn't entered into certain contracts or products that weren't in their best interest. In addition, when faced with someone presenting you with an offer, having an advisor enables you to avoid feeling pressured by saying, "I don't make these decisions without consulting with (trusted advisor name)." If it is a legitimate offer, the person presenting it to you should be happy to discuss it with your accountant, financial advisor, or family member that you rely on.

If you've appropriately accounted for the five things above, your retirement should be in good shape. If you haven't, it may sound overwhelming, but the planning process helps rid you of fear and anxiety. Once you've tackled these things, you can relax and enjoy retirement.

Dreaming of the Future while Living in Today

Okay, let's assume you've tackled or are tackling the issues noted above, what next? My wife and I have moved into the empty-nester phase of our life. At the same time, we still have at least fifteen years in which we plan to work. This brings up two great opportunities for communication with each other:

1. What do we see ourselves doing on a day-to-day basis now that the kids are all out of the house?
2. What dreams do we have for ourselves when we exit full time work?

If you are approaching #1 then I highly recommend you start using some of the time you have together to explore this topic in-depth. My wife and I go to our favorite coffee and bagel shop every Saturday morning. I find it interesting that she gets the same bagel and cream cheese option every week. On the other hand, while I have my favorite standby, I like to experiment with the seasonal bagels and coffees. In many ways, I believe this analogy carries over into how we view life after kids and the retirement years. She plays the role of safe, steady and predictable, while I dream about options 'outside the box.'

In the two general questions above, there can be some overlap, but for the most part, try to split your answers into two groups. I recommend both of you get a small notebook or hardcover diary-type book and jot down your thoughts before you get together. Here are a few questions you might want to reflect upon first and then discuss:

Empty-Nester Questions

1. Make a list of things you've always wanted to do but couldn't because you were busy raising your kids. Have fun with it, these are just ideas. You aren't committed to doing them. Maybe you've wanted to get into photography, writing, or joining the church choir. Anything that interests you… jot it down.

2. Do you want to stay in the same house or move? There is a lot to consider in this question. Mr. Practical (me) might be all for selling, to not have to air condition five bedrooms and take care of an acre yard and pool. On the other hand, Mrs. Hospitality might want to have a place for the kids and eventual grandkids to come back to. Guys, I've already found out that, "they can get a hotel," isn't the best answer.

3. Do you want to do any house renovations? Maybe moving isn't the issue, but you've always wanted to turn that extra bedroom into a man cave. Or maybe you want to blow out a few walls and open up your floor plan and update the kitchen. Question 2 and 3 work in tandem and can come with serious cost increases or decreases.

4. What do you want to do with all the extra money? You might be a semi-empty nester for a few years while your kids are in college, so costs may actually go up with tuition and travel expenses to come home, etc., but at some point your food bill and child rearing expenses should come to an end. As mentioned previously, it was clearly understood in our house that our role was to help best prepare our children for college and then them making it on their own in the real world. For us "boomerang kids" meant visits from well-adjusted kids wanting to share their future family's life with us, not living in an extra bedroom while they "find themselves." Some of the answers to this question might include; paying down the mortgage quicker, setting aside more for retirement, travel, or investing in hobbies.

5. What do you want to do to make sure we get reacquainted? You may not think the kids leaving for college is going to be a big impact on your marriage, but if you track the number of hours your children spend with you or around you during a week, you might be surprised. I had a friend who was depressed about the inevitable arrival of the day when his last child left the nest, but he received some good advice. Someone they knew from church was a few years ahead of them and told him, "My wife and I are dating all over again." He further advised, "Don't be cheap in your dating. Have fun. Travel together. Be spontaneous." After relaying this exchange to me, we decided that since are kids are of similar age, we can work on this together. We both live in different states and our spouses are good friends as well. We've decided to spend the money to get together several times a year and enjoy this chapter in our lives.

Retirement-Dream Questions

1. Should we stay or should we go? No, this isn't a reference to "The Kinks," song, but it is that similar question about staying in the big house or making the move to downsize. One variation I have seen on this theme is selling the big house and buying a smaller house along with a beach condo or mountain cabin.

2. What hobbies do you want to pursue yourself? Writing? Beekeeping? Sewing? Scuba Diving? Car restoration? Antiquing? Beer Brewing? Cooking? Dream big.

3. Do you want to get involved in volunteer work? Do you have a favorite charity? Can you volunteer at your church or synagogue? Are there organizations you like that have overseas mission trips available? What about your local hospital, elementary school, or park?

4. What activities would you enjoy doing together? This could be the volunteer work or possibly an exercise activity to stay fit. Do you have mountains, beaches, springs or parks nearby to walk, bike, swim, hike and explore together?

5. What type of travel would you like to do? One of you might imagine summers spent fly-fishing in a cold mountain lake and winters by the fire reading your favorite books. The other might envision summers playing with the grandchildren in their backyard and winters skiing out west. Put all of your dreams down on paper separately and then come together to chat about it. You may be surprise to learn something new about your mate. Are there activities you can combine? Maybe you can put together a schedule where one year you travel out west to the mountains and another you spend on the islands in the Caribbean.

My wife and I actually had a different twist on this when our kids were young. We listed all the places we'd like to travel with them before they went off to college. Some of these included a vacation to Hawaii, exploring the Northwest; complete with dude ranch, helicopter ride over Glacier National Park, white water rafting and lake trout fishing. We added driving through the covered bridges of Vermont, exploring lighthouses in Maine, and the history of Newport, Rhode Island; to beach vacations in the Caribbean and Mexico, and visiting Niagara Falls and the surrounding area. There were also plans we made and checked off, just for the two of us, to the island of Bermuda and our twenty-fifth anniversary cruise ship vacation to Alaska.

At the beginning of this chapter I asked you if you were squinting in the fog or if the sun was shining bright? By taking time to dream about the future, write down your thoughts and then discuss it together, you can get a clearer picture of what you'd like your future to be. Then with the time you have between now and then you can set aside or reposition assets to make sure that you can realize those dreams. Confidence is key and there is certainly one question, which almost everyone I talk with has a hard time answering.

The most important question to answer is…

Do you know exactly how much money it is going to take for you to retire comfortably and remain comfortable for the rest of your life?

If you are honest and answer "no," then you need to figure it out, so you can plan how to get there. Helping people do this is one of the more satisfying things about what I do.

CHAPTER 12

911 YOU DON'T HAVE TO PANIC!

The best offense is a good defense.

There are dozens of different types of insurance, but before you decide which ones you should or shouldn't have, it's best to understand *why* you purchase insurance in the first place. Insurance should be purchased to transfer risk from you to the insurance company. The question you need to ask yourself before you purchase any type of insurance is, "Will my emergency fund cover me in the event of XYZ disaster?" Insurance is not a pleasant topic to discuss, but it's a necessary one. Once you have the right policies in place you will be able to rest a lot easier.

What insurance is not necessary?

Have you ever been at the cash register to purchase an appliance, computer, or cell phone and have the clerk ask you if you'd like to purchase insurance on the item? Companies make millions of dollars on these policies or they wouldn't offer them, but is it worth buying? If we go back to why you purchase insurance, it is to transfer risk that you wouldn't be able to afford if you suffered a loss. In general, protection of loss or failure on appliances and technology devices are not worth the expense. Most reputable companies will provide you with a short-term return or replacement service for 3-12 months, free of charge. And, if you are following my advice you will have an emergency fund to cover your replacement cost without paying the additional monthly expense for insurance to the company.

I've purchased two flat screen televisions over the past four years and recently an electrical storm put both of them out of commission. I had only owned one of them for four months. I contacted the manufacturer because it was under the initial one year warranty and they fixed it. I couldn't recall how long I had owned my larger flat screen, but knew I had purchased it at Costco, who adds two years onto your one year factory warranty. Unfortunately I found out I was just outside both warranties. I wasn't excited about the idea of dipping into my emergency fund for $1,500, but I knew I had the money to do so. I had watched the repairman fix my first television and asked him if he thought the same part replacement would fix my primary television. He said he thought so and gave me the number for the company's parts department. I ordered the part for $90, looked up how to install it on Youtube, and what do you know, it works!

Other gimmicky insurance policies I would stay away from are cancer insurance and accidental death policies. Many times these are offered through your workplace or through your bank or credit union's third party relationship with another company. These types of policies rarely pay out since they have a specific kind of death requirement. There's a reason they are so cheap. It's better to increase your term life insurance if you think you need a higher death benefit.

Six Must Have Insurance Policies

1. Homeowner's/Renter's
If you have a loan on your house this will normally be a requirement from the bank or mortgage company. They certainly don't want to be on the hook for the loan if your house is destroyed through a fire, tornado, hurricane, or other disaster. Even if you own your house outright, it typical makes sense to carry homeowners to cover one of the most expensive assets you will ever own.

2. Auto
To begin with, driving around uninsured is against the law, but in addition to that the average claim on cars is over $4,000. The most important

aspect of auto insurance is adequate liability coverage. Liability is the insurance that covers anything that you caused in an accident, from damage to the car to the health of anyone in the other car. The minimum amount of insurance most experts recommend is 100/300 limits of bodily injury liability. This means coverage of $100,000 for one person and $300,000 for all people injured in one accident. If you have a significant net worth in which someone might sue you for higher amounts, you might want to consider an umbrella policy (see below). The collision coverage portion of your policy is the amount that pays for your car if it's damaged or destroyed in a wreck. To save money, you can drop your collision or raise your deductible. This would definitely be worth considering if you drive an older car. Just make sure you have enough money in your emergency fund to cover the damages to your car or replace your car it it's totaled.

3.   Health

Most people get their health coverage through their place of employment. If this is you, you may have several options to choose from at different price points. Remember, insurance is used to transfer risk you can't cover on your own. Do you really need a health insurance policy that allows you to pay $10 copays to see the doctor? Your monthly premium is significantly higher to have this feature. You can save hundreds of dollars a month for a plan with a high deductible. Yes, you have to pay for all your doctor visits during the year, except for an annual physical, but if you are in good health you probably don't go very often anyway. What you need health insurance for are the unexpected health issues. I was in perfect health when I was rushed to the hospital with a fever, which turned out to be a bacterial infection in my heart, requiring open-heart surgery to replace my aortic valve. The bill was $90,000 and I was fully covered after my $1,500 deductible. I had the $1,500 in my emergency fund, but not $90,000.

If you don't have a plan at work then you still have other options available to you. If you are a small business owner with at least two employees, you can set up your own group plan with guaranteed coverage. If you are an individual, you can access a government plan under the Affordable Care Act. In addition, there are also numerous health care sharing ministries (HCSM) available. HCSMs provide a health care cost sharing arrangement among persons of similar and sincerely held beliefs. The largest ones operating in the United States, covering over 500,000 people, include Samaritan Ministries, Medi-Share, Christian Healthcare Ministries and Liberty Healthshare. Each of them has different requirements to join, but offer very affordable coverage for individuals and families.

4. Disability

Disability insurance covers you in the event you lose your livelihood due to an accident or health issues. How long will your emergency fund last if you could no longer work? By far, the least expensive place to purchase disability coverage is through your company. The two most common policies are short-term and long-term disability. The first one covers you for the first 90 days and the second one picks up after that. If your emergency fund can take you through the first three months then you could just purchase long-term disability. Typically the maximum amount you can purchase is 65% of your current income, which will pay until age 65. You should try to purchase a policy that pays if you can't perform the job that is required of you. This is known as own occupation or own occ. If you are a dentist and can't perform the daily duties in your office, you don't want an insurance company refusing to pay you disability because you can go into teaching dentistry or some other position.

5. Life

Again, like all insurance you need to look at the transfer of risk. In the case of life insurance you need to ask the question, who is going to be impacted monetarily if I pass away unexpectedly? The second question is, how much money, in a lump sum, will it take to replace my loss?

Unlike disability insurance, which is cheaper through your company, most of the time it is cheaper to purchase an individual life insurance policy. Group life insurance is guaranteed to be issued at your place of work, but it is issued at a standard rating. Insurance companies make money on those who are healthy and potentially lose money on those who aren't. If you are healthy, you can get a preferred or preferred plus rating on an individual policy on your own. In addition, you can purchase a 10, 20 or even 30 year guaranteed level-term policy and pay the same premium every year. Group life policies increase in price with your age. In addition, when you leave your job your policy typically will not transfer with you. This is not an issue with an individual policy.

How much life insurance should you purchase? The general rule of thumb is 5 to 10 times your annual salary. To be more specific, consider those dependent upon your income. If you purchase $1,000,000 in coverage and invest it at 5% then that will produce $50,000 a year without touching the principal. For those with young children, you might want to carry more to cover college expenses, pay off debt, or retire a mortgage. For those men who mistakenly think just because their wife doesn't work and stays home with the children, that they don't need life insurance on them, think again. There is a huge value associated with a stay at home parent. Price out what it would cost to pay someone to care for your children while you work and you will see what I mean.

So now that you've come up with the amount, the next question is what type of insurance should you purchase? The cheapest life insurance to purchase is term life. Through a group life policy at work this is done on an annual basis with the premium typically increasing with your age. For an individual term life policy you will typically purchase it for a specific number of years – 10, 15, 20 and 30 are the most common – with a fixed "level" price for each year. Term insurance will provide you with the most amount of coverage for the lowest cost, but there is a reason it is cheaper. Most term life insurance policies never end up paying the death benefit because they only cover you for a specific period of time and then end. Then again, the reason you need insurance of any kind is to cover unexpected and expensive events. Term life insurance is great to cover you for an unexpected passing while your children are growing up. It can provide a spouse with money for loss of income and college costs. As I've mentioned previously, you might want to consider a policy that comes with a conversion feature which allows you to convert the policy from term to permanent insurance in the event you have health issues that come up and make you uninsurable for a new policy in the future.

The other broad category of life insurance is permanent. Its name represents the fact that if you pay the premiums then eventually it will pay off when you die (yes, I know I used the politically incorrect terminology, die versus passing. But *passing* sounds like I'm playing football). With permanent life insurance you are essentially paying for the term insurance, but also sending in additional premium that is invested in a fixed account with the insurance company (whole life or universal life) or mutual funds (variable life). These extra dollars grow and help pay for the future term insurance within the policy that will be much more expensive in later years. For the majority, term insurance will make the most sense, but for those with significant income, where they have already maxed out their retirement plans, permanent insurance can be a way to set aside additional money for tax-free retirement income. There also may be ways you can utilize permanent insurance for estate tax purposes. These are important concepts to discuss with a Financial Planner, CPA, and Estate Planning Attorney.

6. Long-term Care

Between the ages of 55-66 years old, you should consider looking into long-term care insurance. In 2012, the average cost of a private room in a nursing home was more than $90,000 a year. That can crack and scramble a nest egg in a heartbeat. You may not be at this stage of life yet, but your parents could be, so think about having them look into the options available in their state. Many people mistakenly believe that Medicare will cover long-term care expenses. Most long-term care isn't medical care, but rather assistance with basic personal tasks of everyday life, sometimes referred to as activities of daily living or ADLs. The six ADLs include (1) bathing; (2) continence; (3) dressing; (4) eating; (5) toileting and (6) transferring. Most long term care policies will pay benefits when you cannot do 2 out of 6 of the activities. The definition of each of these, are as follows:

> **Bathing** – Washing yourself by sponge bath; or in either a tub or shower, including the process of getting into and/or out of the tub or shower.

> **Continence** – Ability to maintain control of bowel and bladder functions; or when unable to maintain control of bowel or

bladder functions, the ability to perform associated personal hygiene.

Dressing – Putting on and taking off all items of clothing and any necessary braces, fasteners or artificial limbs. This includes buttoning buttons and tying shoes.

Eating – Ability to, without the aid of another person, maintain an adequate food and fluid intake consistent with dietary needs.

Toileting – Getting to and from the toilet, getting on and off the toilet and performing associated personal hygiene.

Transferring – Moving into or out of a bed, chair or wheelchair. Transferring does not include the task of getting into or out of the tub or shower.

While some companies may have group long term care (LTC) policies available as a benefits option for employees, most claims do not take place until after age 70, when you have probably stopped working. The three main types of individual long term care policies are (1) traditional LTC policy; (2) life insurance with an LTC rider and (3) Hybrid single premium policies. You should consult an objective financial advisor to thoroughly understand which option is best for you, but here are a few of the nuances of each:

Traditional Long Term Care Insurance – With this type of policy you elect your benefits at the outset:

1. Monthly Benefit (typical range of $3,000 - $15,000)
2. Benefit Period (2, 3, 4, 5, 6, 10 years, or Unlimited) (Individual or Shared)
3. Inflation Protection (3% Compound, 5% Simple, 5% Compound)
4. Waiting Period (30 days, 60 days, 90 days)

The premium will increase depending upon how benefit rich your policy is. The younger you are when you start the policy the less expensive the premium. The policy is guaranteed renewable, but the premium isn't guaranteed not to increase in the future. Like your auto, homeowners and disability policy, there is no cash value built up. So at the end of the day, if you don't use the insurance then all the premiums you paid out are gone.

Life insurance with an LTC rider – Essentially this is a life insurance policy that allows you to access your death benefit in advance for long-term care needs. So in essence you are spending down the death benefit for a beneficiary while you are living and have increased expenses. Depending upon your health, it may be an option to get this type of policy if you don't qualify for a traditional LTC policy. The underwriters for life insurance want you to live a long time and the underwriters for long term care want you to die quickly. Well, the underwriter doesn't personally have something out for you, but that is the way they look at the condition of your health. Yes, it's a little morbid, but it's the truth.

Hybrid Single Premium Policies – Unlike traditional policies that have a monthly or annual premium "pay as you go" approach, this type of policy is usually funded with a one-time single premium up-front, such as $50,000 or $100,000. Many hybrid policies also provide you the ability to elect your LTC benefits at the outset, i.e. monthly benefit, benefit period, and inflation protection. The waiting period will be fixed by the insurance company and is typically 90 days or less.

The appeal of hybrid long term care life insurance policies is that you are guaranteed to receive your premium back should you never need to receive long term care. Also, premiums with these policies are fixed, and are guaranteed to never be increased.

I like to say that these are win-win-win policies. Although the winner might not actually be you, it might be your beneficiary. Regardless, there are 3 outcomes with these policies:

1. The policy pays for your LTC costs should you receive care (the monthly maximum and total benefits paid are based upon the initial lump sum you deposit, age, gender and other factors).
2. Provide your beneficiary with a tax-free life insurance benefit if you pass away prior to needing care.

3. Return your lump sum premium if you change your mind and decide you want it back.

If you have assets set aside in a money market account or CDs, that you are not using for retirement then you could simply reposition those assets to leverage your dollars for LTC. Let's say you are 60 years old and have $500,000 set aside in savings, which you've thought you might use for long-term care or other health needs in the future if you need it. You might *reposition* $100,000 of these assets into a Hybrid Policy. In doing so you could receive:

- $500,000 of long term care benefits ($7,000 a month for 6 years) should you need care,
- $165,000 tax-free life insurance benefit to your beneficiary should you pass away prematurely, or
- $100,000 returned to you should you change your mind and want or need your money back.

This would then allow you to put the other $400,000 you had set aside for LTC and health issues to work somewhere else.

Two Other Insurance Policies You Should Consider

1. Umbrella Insurance
Umbrella insurance is typically purchased through the company that insures your house or cars. It is designed to help protect you from major claims and lawsuits and as a result it protects or puts an *umbrella* over your assets. You need to read the details of any policies you are considering, but here are two ways an umbrella policy may protect you:

A. Provides additional liability coverage above the limits of your homeowners, auto, and boat insurance policies. This protection is designed to kick in when the liability on these other policies has been exhausted.

B. Provides coverage for claims that may be excluded by other liability policies including: false arrest, libel, slander, and liability coverage on rental units you own.

An example of how this might work is as follows. Let's say you were found guilty of causing an auto accident and the cost of the injuries you caused to others is $500,000. Let's further assume that the Bodily Injury limit on your auto insurance is $300,000. Your auto policy will cover $300,000 of the injuries, but who will cover the remaining $200,000? Your umbrella policy might. The right policy should cover the amount above the limit set in your auto policy, up to the limit you choose for your umbrella policy. A $1,000,000 umbrella policy is actually quite affordable as it works with your other policies and in this case with your auto policy there is essentially a $300,000 deductible before the umbrella policy kicks in.

2. Identity Theft Insurance

The 2012 Javelin Strategy & Research Report determined that 11.6 million people became a victim of identity theft in the United States in 2011.[1] With criminals becoming more and more sophisticated, the numbers are only increasing. This could happen when someone steals your driver's license, there is a data breach at a big chain store, or when you use your credit card on-line. Whatever the case, it's a smart move to protect yourself with the right theft protection. There are a number of companies that provide theft insurance. Make sure when you get a quote that the insurance includes *restoration services* which assign a qualified counselor to clean up the mess. The insurance does not reimburse you for assets that you might lose to identity theft, but rather they reimburse you for expenses you might incur in restoring your identity and credit. It also saves you the time and aggravation of doing this yourself.

CHAPTER 13

GIVING IT AWAY

You never saw a hearse pulling a U-haul.

To start this chapter, I wanted to provide you with some of my favorite quotes on living a balanced life with my commentary after each.

"He is no fool who gives what he cannot keep to gain what he cannot lose." Jim Elliot

Jim was a Christian who was one of five missionaries killed while participating in Operation Auca, an attempt to evangelize the Huaorani Indians of Ecuador. You can read the amazing story of his life in, "Gates of Splendor," or watch the movie, "End of the Spear." The spiritual connotations of his quote are profound.

"The love of money is the root of all kinds of evil." I Timothy 6:10

One of the most misquoted verses of all time. I see it quoted on television and in print frequently, as "money is the root of all evil." Money is an inanimate object. It is neither good nor bad. Money can be used to help someone in need. Or you can spend eighty hours a week trying to get rich versus spending time with your family. The *love* or pursuit of it at all costs is what makes the difference.

"When the game is over the King and Pawn both go back into the same box." Italian Proverb

Great quote. No matter what station you are in life, rich or poor, everyone dies in the end. Everyone has the same 24 hours a day, 7 days a week, 365 days a year. Linda Ellis, the author of the poem, "The Dash," makes the point another way. Between the year of your birth and death, on your tombstone, there is a dash. This small line represents all the days of your life. In the end, what did you do with your *dash* or time? Did you make a difference to those around you?

Why is death important to money? When you consider death, and its finality, you're forced to think of what is truly important. We get so comfortable with waking up each day, getting ready, doing the normal things, making some money, coming home, and starting the process over.

One day, that cycle will be broken, and all the things you did in life, and all the accomplishments will not have mattered.

Like I said in the subtitle of this chapter, you won't be escorted by a U-Haul after you die. It is easy to be blinded by all the fancy and amazing things this world has to offer, but then your means and your end become indecipherable. When you first enter the work force, you earn money for the sake of earning money.

It starts out innocently enough, maybe you're earning money to:

- Get through college.
- Take care of your family.
- Buy a nice car.
- Get a bigger house.
- Have financial stability.

All of those are perfectly normal reasons to earn money, but what do they yield? Are you going to college to earn more money, or are you going to college to do what you love? Will the nicer car cost you more money in maintenance, gas, etc? Will the bigger house require you to work more to maintain, heat, cool, and pay the taxes? Is that all life is about? There is a quote that says, "He who dies with the most toys wins," but I would say, "He who dies with the most toys, still dies."

"Then he said to them, "Watch out! Be on your guard against all kinds of greed; life does not consist in an abundance of possessions." And he told them this parable: "The ground of a certain rich man yielded an abundant harvest. He thought to himself, 'What shall I do? I have no place to store my crops.' "Then he said, 'This is what I'll do. I will tear down my barns and build bigger ones, and there I will store my surplus grain. And I'll say to myself, "You have plenty of grain laid up for many years. Take life easy; eat, drink and be merry."' "But God

said to him, 'You fool! This very night your life will be demanded from you. Then who will get what you have prepared for yourself?' "This is how it will be with whoever stores up things for themselves but is not rich toward God." Luke 12:15-21

Sometimes there is this unvoiced assumption that we will live forever, but in the deep recesses of our mind we know that someday it will all come to an end. We just don't want to deal with it. And, while like money, growing a business is not a bad thing, in and of itself; the issue is how we deal with the process. If the plans for my life are interrupted prematurely, will I consider my relationships with my family, friends, and my God a success? King David answers the question from the previous parable.

"Do not be overawed when a man grows rich, when the splendor of his house increases; for he will take nothing with him when he dies, his splendor will not descend with him. Though while he lived he counted himself blessed—and men praise you when you prosper—he will join the generation of his fathers, who will never see the light 'of life." Psalm 49:16-19

Again, you can't take it with you, so what are you going to do with it?

"Whoever loves money never has enough; whoever loves wealth is never satisfied with his income. This too is meaningless. As goods increase, so do those who consume them. And what benefit are they to the owner except to feast his eyes on them? The sleep of a laborer is sweet, whether he eats little or much, but the abundance of a rich man permits him no sleep. I have seen a grievous evil under the sun: wealth hoarded to the harm of its owner, or wealth lost through some misfortune... Naked a man comes from his mother's womb, and as he comes, so he departs..." Ecclesiastes 5:10-15

The famous, naked a man comes from his mother's womb, and naked he will return quote, comes from King Solomon, who is purported to be the wisest man who ever lived. If you read through the book of Ecclesiastes, you will become privy to the writings of the King of Israel towards the end of his life. He discusses in great detail, his personal experiences through life. Everything he sought was out of a desire to find *pleasure and meaning.* Some things never change. Over 2,500 years later many people are still in pursuit of the same euphoric goal. Solomon determined that all of his efforts to find happiness were *"vanity and striving after the wind."*

The king then lamented that he hated everything he had built because, *"seeing that I must leave it to the man who will come after me, and who knows whether he will be wise or a fool? Yet he will be master of all for which I toiled and used my wisdom* (to build)." Ecclesiastes 2:18-19. His concern was over whether his heirs were going to be wise or foolish with what he passed along to them?

A number of years ago, I met with some wealthy, out of town clients at their home. They surprised me by having four additional people at the dining room table who were interested in asking some financial questions. One woman was a little unnerving to me. She wore dark sunglasses the entire time (we were inside) and didn't ask a single question. After a few hours, we finished up and as I was gathering my things, the mysterious woman approached me.

"Would you mind meeting with my son today?" she asked.

"I'm headed back home," I responded, "But why don't you tell me a little about him and why you'd like me to meet with him?"

I hedged my situation, both intrigued, but also knowing I had a family waiting for me and not wanting to waste my time. I wasn't expecting her response.

"My son is nineteen, his father passed away and he's one of the heirs to the XYZ Company. He has four trusts that pay him regularly and he's spending two to three hundred thousand dollars a month."

You don't have to be a Finance major to quickly calculate in your head that if someone is spending $250,000 a month, they must have a serious income.

"Sure, I think I can make time to do that?" I told her.

I followed her across town to a road that paralleled the Atlantic Ocean. Eventually we pulled up to a gate. The woods on the property near the road blocked a view of the house. I followed her down a long driveway, we parked and then she led me past a nine car garage. The doors were all open and I marveled at one exotic car after another – Ferrari, Lamborghini, Bentley, and on and on. There were nine, highly polished cars in total.

The one story house ran hundreds of feet along the Atlantic shoreline. We entered and walked down a dimly lit hallway that opened up into a large room. Eight flat screen monitors were stacked, four on top of four. Eight different images were lit up. A few of them were financial websites, another was CNBC, and a fourth had a music video running. I couldn't readily take in the other four. Her son spun around in his chair with a Red Bull can in hand. There was a brief, awkward introduction and then she announced, "I'll leave the two of you alone to chat." Then she was gone.

As I started with a brief introduction of myself, a large man walked into the room and sat down on a coach, next to us. I wasn't sure if he was a body guard or another relative. *Later on he introduced himself as a neighbor and ironically liked what I had to say and became a client himself.*

Back to the trust baby.

With the eight screens flashing different information and amped up on Red Bull, he didn't seem to focus much on what I was saying. I tried to find out more about his spending habits, more about the family fortune and what he wanted to be when he grew up. That seemed to hit a nerve as he confessed about blowing through crazy amounts of money each month, yet deep down inside he wanted to be able to prove to people around him that he could be a valued, contributing member to the family business.

Just when I thought we were getting somewhere, he jumped up and decided to give me a tour. On the way out to the yacht, I think I was most impressed with the .50 caliber machine gun. After the tour, he said he had to go, but wanted to get back together and have me provide him with a proposal for investing a small amount of money (small in relation to his family's fortune).

We had a few interactions via e-mail and the phone before I returned to South Florida for a second visit. Through our erratic communication, it became clear to me that he was not going to be the type of client I'd want to work with. I didn't feel that he could focus on a concrete goal, I was unsure of his ethical behavior, and I didn't think he would act on the unvarnished advice I would give him. When we sat down by his eight screens, the conversation went something like this.

"So, what do you have for me?"

I pulled my Bible out and opened to Ecclesiastes. "Have you heard of King Solomon?" I asked.

"No."

"He was the wisest man who ever lived."

I watched as he typed, *King Solomon*, into Wikipedia, to verify what I was saying. Then I continued.

"The king was also the richest man who had ever lived. And you know what his biggest concern was?"

He leaned forward. "What?"

"He hated everything he had built because, he realized he was going to have to leave it to someone who would come after him and he didn't know whether that person would be wise with it or a fool?"

I seemed to have his attention, so I concluded.

"Your father built up a huge estate and you are inheriting a lot of money. You are the person the king was worrying about. Are you going to be wise with this money or a fool?"

I can say with a great deal of certainty that he wasn't anticipating what I was delivering. I think he expected most people to tell him what he *wanted* to hear to try and get his business. I told him what he *needed* to hear and wasn't trying to get his business. I wish I could say there was a happy ending to this story, but he didn't become a client and that was our last serious conversation. I like to think that if he ever reflects on conversations people have had with him, he will remember what I told him that day and it will be of benefit.

I work with estate planning attorneys to help clients craft documents for those that will inherit their wealth. We cover a lot of important questions and family issues to try and make the transition smooth and be a benefit to the heirs versus a hindrance. I have concluded that training children from a young age to be responsible with money is more effective than trying to control everything from the grave, through estate documents.

If you've never read the book of Ecclesiastes, I highly recommend it. It's not a long book, but there is a lot of relevant content. Fortunately in the book's final two verses, Solomon provides his answer to life's pursuit of pleasure dilemma. I won't spoil it for you here.

In his book of Proverbs, Solomon concluded:

"Wealth is worthless in the day of wrath, but righteousness delivers from death… Whoever trusts in his riches will fall… Proverbs 11:4,28

It begs the question. If we can't trust in our money and the false security it brings, what can we trust in?

There are really only two options. If you believe your time on earth is all there is and after that it's *ashes to ashes and dust to dust,* then Paul gives guidance in I Corinthians 15:32. *"Eat, drink and be merry for tomorrow we may die."*

If on the other hand you believe there is life after death, then logically only two things survive, God and people's souls, therefore invest your time in both. This can take on many forms, but includes giving through your time, talent, and treasure. Actions could include helping a widow with repairs on her house, taking your family on a mission trip to help orphans in another country, or giving money to organizations that assist the needy in your local area.

One of the best decisions my wife and I made, was to have our entire family go on a trip to Bolivia, where we built relationships with fifty boys' in an orphanage, assisted in work projects around the compound, and went out into the neighboring villages for Sidewalk Sunday School time with 50 – 300 children at a time. It was an eye-opener for all of us, to experience first-hand the conditions others live in around the world.

In the book, "Into Thin Air," author Jon Krakauer, recounts the true story of the most disastrous Mount Everest expedition in history. Interestingly, the climax of the story does not occur upon reaching the mountain's peak, but instead it occurs in the storm on the descent.

I like to relate this story to someone's financial life. Most of the financial services industry is focused on helping clients build their wealth. Setting goals and reaching them, like the mountain climbers reaching the summit. But in many ways the descent can be much more daunting.

- How much money is safe to withdraw so you don't run out?
- Is it better to take from taxable accounts, IRA's, Roth IRA, cash value life insurance or annuities first?
- When should you start taking social security?
- When should you start taking money from a pension?
- How do I handle unexpected medical costs and health issues that arise?

How much you withdraw and how you do so, can make a significant difference, from both a current income tax standpoint and the wealth you choose to give to your heirs and charity after you are gone. If your goal is to maximize what you pass to your heirs then it's better to spend down assets where you pay current income taxes versus those you will get a step-up in basis at death. Other assets are better to leave to charity. The cost to find competent advisors to help coordinate your retirement, estate, and charitable giving issues is miniscule in comparison to what the expenses could be in *winging it* on your own.

CHAPTER 14

LOOKING BEHIND THE CURTAIN

10 Things Financial Advisors Don't Want You to Know.[1]

One premise I tell my clients up front is, "Don't believe anyone who tells you they are totally objective. Everyone has biases. The important thing is to understand what biases exist with each professional, and then determine if they are acceptable." My best qualification for writing this article is that I've been compensated every way you can be as a financial planner: commission-only, fee-only, and fee-based (fees and commissions). Clearly these 10 things don't apply to every advisor, but hopefully they'll provide some insights to help you know what to watch for:

1. "The title on my business card may not mean much." Company names and individual titles have changed rapidly in recent years. Companies have changed the ending of their name from XYZ Life Insurance Company to the XYZ Financial Group or XYZ Wealth Management. There are many examples of this, and it isn't by accident. Most of these companies operate the same way they used to, but have added additional products and want to be perceived as more than just insurance companies. Individual titles have also changed. Gone are the days of the stockbroker, life insurance agent, or registered representative. They have been replaced by wealth manager, financial advisor or financial planner. Read the list again. Sure, they convey professional counsel, but has anything really changed besides the title?

2. "The financial service I'm selling is only a sideline for my company." From a marketing and profitability standpoint, banks and accounting firms joining the ranks of "financial advisors" makes a lot of sense. Whether it's a good thing for consumers is another matter. Traditionally people have trusted bankers and accountants for independent advice. But now that banks offer to handle your investments, insurance, estate issues, 401(k), and so on, it's no longer safe to automatically regard their advice as unbiased. It isn't uncommon to be talking with the teller at your bank and have them bring up the fact that you have a large balance in your savings account and then be asked if you want to step down the hall to their "advisor" who can assist you in investing your money. Almost every time I contact my insurance company/bank (a large well known company that caters to military members and veterans); I am asked if I would like to have a financial advisor contact me to help with my planning. CPA's are the largest group moving into financial planning products. There's danger in having consumers expecting one type of service and then being cross-sold into areas outside the bank's or CPA's core competencies. One-stop shoppers may appreciate this, but you need to make sure you're only getting the services you need and desire.

3. "I want your will and trust on file because I make my real money on the settlement of your estate." Passing the bar exam does not mean an attorney is competent in estate planning. This is a highly specialized area where the law is constantly changing. Misleading seminar headlines cause many people to believe "no probate = no fees." Not so. Even with a trust, up to 5% of your estate can go to an attorney and trustee for administration and settlement fees.

4. "The shell game I play with class A, B, C and I shares is more to my advantage than yours." If you choose to utilize a broker to buy mutual funds, their compensation differs based on what class of shares you buy.

- "A shares" typically have a high front-end load and average annual management fees.
- "B shares" move the load from the front to the back, meaning you only pay it if you cash out within a short time, usually five

years. The broker gets paid by the fund organization rather than your front-end load, so the fund organization makes it up by charging you higher than usual annual management fees. Most companies have moved away from B shares, due to some brokers presenting them as no-load funds while not fully explaining the back-end surrender charges.

- "C shares" have no front-end load, low or no back-end loads, but the highest annual expenses of the four classes.
- "I shares" are an institutional share class and have no front-end loads and typically have the lowest annual expenses of the four classes.

None of these share classes is wrong per-se and there are even Z shares and others popping up now. If you choose to use a broker, they need to be compensated. But you need to know which shares you are getting, and for what reason. Which class is the best deal usually depends on how long you hold the shares of that fund, something your broker should be able and willing to explain to you.

5. "I'm learning as I go." Financial planning has become a hot profession over the past few decades. The trouble is, due to the low barrier to entry (passing an insurance and investment exam); many sales people without experience or formal financial training call themselves "financial planners." Some of these people sell investment and insurance products without fully understanding the tax, retirement, and estate ramifications. Instead of focusing on what you really need and why, the sales pitch becomes "mine's cheaper" or "has better performance than theirs." After the 2008 market meltdown, the government has developed more regulations and requirements for financial firms to try and create more transparency for the public.

Here are some relevant questions for each category of planner:

- Fee-only planners: Most provide asset management services. Do they offer choices? Are they locked into doing it only one way? Many in this group tend to have limited knowledge of insurance related products and how they work.

- Fee-based planners: Are they loyal to one insurance or invest-ment company? Do they "push" their company's products in their recommendations? Can they do fee planning without products?
- Commission planners: My first year in the business was in this group and I wouldn't rely on this group for serious financial planning. They can however be excellent for individual prod-ucts, if you already know what you need.

6. "I'm being paid more to sell you certain products." Early in my career I learned about wholesalers. Their job is to influence planners to sell their company's funds or insurance products by helping the planner understand how the products work, providing illustration support, and expediting delivery of the product. At one point I was in a presentation where a company was offering three fixed annuity options. Each had a first year guaranteed interest rate that changed to an estimated renewal projection (see table below).

Guaranteed Rate 1st Year	Projected Renewal Rate	Commission to Agent
9.50%	6.25%	4.00%
7.50%	6.25%	6.00%
7.10%	5.85%	8.00%

The wholesaler told the planners to present whichever option they wanted to. There's clearly a conflict here: the best product for the client results in the worst commission for the planner. To be fair, I have found some wholesalers to be an excellent resource for detailed information on their funds or products. I just make it a point to contact the ones whose funds I already use after doing my own personal due diligence.

7. "The level of attention I give you depends on how I'm paid." Fortunately the days of trading commissions are drawing to a close. Under this old scenario, the broker was paid to buy and sell your stocks. The question then was, "Is this recommendation in my best interest or is my broker just trying to make a commission?" Most brokerage companies and advisors have been moving to an "assets under management" (AUM) fee, which allows for unlimited trading. Problem solved? Perhaps. But a new question has surfaced: Is there a bias to collect assets and then do nothing? A valid question, since the advisor gets paid regardless of whether he does anything with your account or not. While the new method is preferable, be aware of the possibility of being ignored, and find out what you are getting for the fee being charged. Is the advisor actually managing your assets or does he pass along this duty to a third party investment firm that adds on an additional layer of fees? Are you getting extras like quarterly meetings, annual updates of a net worth statement, and basic tax, retirement, and estate planning?

8. "My promise to get you a better return than you're getting now is empty." Be wary of anyone who makes this claim. Not only can't they guarantee it, it's not legal to do so. Understand that an appeal to you based upon returns is preying on your emotions, specifically fear and greed. Promises during a booming economy are easy to fulfill. When the market goes down it's another story. I typically gain more new business when the market goes down, as people find out they aren't Warren Buffet, and realize they haven't utilized some of the investment options, like diversification, limit orders, and asset rotation to try and limit their downside risk. Don't base your investing on how many stars a fund has, historical returns, or promises. A consistent investment strategy based upon your goals, risk threshold, and timeframe is critical.

9. "My comprehensive financial plan is just a way for me to discover what other assets you have to invest." Some financial advisors offer to do "planning" for free, since their profit is in the products they sell. Often this translates into selling a "cookie cutter" plan—your information is sent to company headquarters, and generic recommendations for that company's products are returned. To quote a stockbroker friend of mine who used to work at one of the largest brokerage houses: "Our financial plans are really designed to reveal more of our client's assets to invest." Ouch. If you have significant estate, tax, and investment issues and want professional advice, don't try to save a buck by paying a nominal fee for advice. No one works for free. In the end, your cost will probably be about the same, but the objectivity of the advice you get may be very different.

10. "You don't really need my help with your investing." I like to joke that "financial planning is not rocket-surgery." But it can be confusing and time consuming as laws and products continually evolve. Just like most services you may need in life, except for "brain surgery" or "rocket science," you can probably teach yourself, but do you want to take the time to do so? Not only is time an issue but how are your emotions going to hold up as you manage your retirement nest egg during a market downturn? One of the more difficult issues is integrating your investing with the other areas of your financial picture—taxes, estate, retirement, college planning, etc.—to find the most effective mix. Some people are intimidated by the technical issues of investing. Others want to off-load the stress and emotions of investing to someone they can trust. Just remember, planning is a process, not an event. You don't evaluate your situation one time at age 35 and then consider yourself done. The issues in growing your wealth are very different from the point of retirement and switching to how best to withdraw your assets and make them last a lifetime. Either way you need to continually review your financial health, especially if you're managing it unassisted.

CHAPTER 15

LOOK BEFORE YOU LEAP!

How to choose an advisor.

I f you are looking for a financial advisor to help you reach your goals, one of the best places to start is with friends and family. You should get recommendations from people whose financial needs, outlook or station in life is similar to yours. Before contacting the advisor you can get additional background on social media pages, like LinkedIn or Facebook, to get a sense of what each firm is like. You could also try to meet the advisor in more of a social setting, through a monthly function they might be having. Our firm has a unique venue, topic or experience each month and invites clients to bring friends. It's a great way to meet an advisor without the pressure of an office visit.

You can also search for a planner directly at www.CFP.net, which is the Certified Financial Planner® website. Most advisors also have their own website. If friends and family have recommended a few names, you can visit the advisors website to obtain details about their firm, their personal background and the types of clients they work with.

If you are looking for a well-rounded advisor who can provide advice in a variety of areas then I would recommend choosing a Certified Financial Planner Practicioner®. Unlike most certifications in the financial services industry that require minimal effort to obtain, the CFP® certification typical takes two years of study, followed by a two day exam, with a pass rate of just 50%.

Once you have a list of potential advisors, take one more step before setting up appointments to meet: Find out whether they have ever been disciplined for unlawful or unethical behavior. You can do this using the Financial Industry Regulatory Authority's (FINRA) broker check at www.brokercheck.finra.org.

10 Questions to ask in your initial interview

1. How do you charge for your financial planning services?

There are three main ways to charge for financial planning services and as I have mentioned, I have worked in all three. Typically, commission-only is more product-oriented since something has to be sold for the advisor to be compensated. This may be appropriate for you if you know you want a specific insurance or annuity product or are buying individual stocks or bonds you want to hold for an extended period of time.

Most people looking for in-depth financial planning, recommendations, and implementation will seek out a fee-only advisor or a fee & commission advisor. Over my career I have provided the same advice under both compensation structures. I chose to move away from a fee-only model because I felt it limited my ability to provide implementation services. For instance, if I recommended a term life insurance policy or long-term care insurance, I want to be able to go out on behalf of my client and find the most cost effective policies with the best features, instead of sending them on their way with the recommendation. They might end up having an agent steer them towards one company's product, which may not be in the client's best interest.

Ask if the advisor charges by the hour, plan or period of time for their planning services. Again, I have charged all three ways. My preferred method is to charge a one-time annual fee that includes a plan, recommendations, and help implementing the recommendations my client decides to move ahead with over the course of the year. I like this format because the client knows what the cost is. There are no hidden fees, additional costs for phone calls, meetings, or coordinating implementation with other advisors (like CPAs or attorneys). At the end of the year we can access where we have come and if it makes sense to continue working on a reduced retainer for ongoing advice. I would steer clear of someone who says they do planning for *free*. Everyone knows that nothing comes free. The advisor's incentive will be to steer you towards products in which they will get paid or pressure you to move your investments to them.

2. What is the total cost for your asset management services?
This is a great question because if you frame it this way you might get some insight into how transparent an advisor is. There are many fees in the financial services industry (see Chapter 14 on *10 Things Financial Advisors Don't Want You to Know*). While fees themselves are not inherently bad, since advisors need to be paid for their services, it is important to know what they are:

Asset Management Fee – This is the fee the advisor charges for their services and splits with the broker-dealer they are aligned with. If the advisor is an individual RIA (Registered Investment Advisor), then they may keep the entire fee. On a side note, if an advisor is their own RIA then you will want to ask additional questions on reporting and Errors and Omission insurance. If the advisor generates their own statements then there is less oversight than if the statements come from a third party source. In addition, if there was ever a reason to take legal action against the advisor you want to make sure they have an insurance policy to back them up.

Getting back to the asset management fee, this is typically an annual fee, deducted monthly or quarterly from your account, based upon the level of assets being managed. Typically the more assets being managed the lower the asset management fee will go. The benefit to this type of fee arrangement, versus a commission, is that all assets are the same and there is no incentive to sell a specific investment or make changes just to generate more commissions (or loads).

If the advisor you are interviewing says, "I charge an asset management fee of one percent," and then stops. I recommend asking the question again, "Is that *the total cost* for asset management services?" If they answer yes, then ask; "What about internal expenses (expense ratios) on the investments you use?" Followed up by; "Are there any third party expenses?"

Individual stocks do not have expense ratios, but all mutual funds and exchange traded funds do. These are part of your total cost. Ask which types of investment the advisor will use in the recommended portfolio.

One advisor may use mutual funds with average internal expenses of 1.25%, while another may use exchange traded funds with average internal expenses of .25%. That 1% difference is in addition to the 1% asset management fee they may charge. In real money that is potentially a $1,000 annual difference on every $100,000 being managed.

Third party expenses – In addition to the asset management fee to the advisor and internal expenses of the investments utilized, there are many advisors who engage a third party to do the investing for them. This can add up to an additional 1% fee.

Volume discounts – As I mentioned previously, most advisors will reduce their fees as your assets grow. For instance, your fee could be one rate from $100,000 - $999,000 and then drop at $1,000,000. **The important question to ask is**, "Do you use a blended reduction for each additional dollar or do you reduce the fees back to the first dollar?" There is a big difference. In the first scenario your fee may be 1.25% up to $999,000 and then drop to 1% after $1,000,000. If you invest $1,100,000, the reduction to 1% is only on the additional $100,000, but if the advisor reduces the fee back to the first dollar, then the 1% is charged on the entire $1,100,000. That difference in fees to you is $2,500 a year. Unfortunately, my experience is that most prospective clients who talk to me have never had this clearly explained up front by an advisor.

3. What do you actually do for the asset management fees?

As I mentioned in Chapter 9, there are a lot of "financial advisors" who I describe as *asset gatherers*. They ask a number of risk tolerance questions and then recommend one of 8-10 portfolios managed by a third party. While they have performed a service in regards to helping you determine which asset allocation might be appropriate based upon historical returns and volatility, their involvement in the investment process after this is limited. They can even check a box to have the portfolio automatically reallocated periodically for you. Their real service is helping you stay on track with your goals by making changes to your allocation over time.

The ultimate issue is feeling that you are getting good value, which is the relationship between fees and services. I like to do this by reducing my fees to first dollar, as mentioned in question 2. Second, by proactively managing the portfolio myself so there are no third party fees. And third, by utilizing Exchange Traded Index Funds (ETFs), which have much lower internal expenses than mutual funds. From a true management standpoint, I monitor the ETFs I recommend daily and make changes monthly as necessary based upon my relative strength rotation strategy. In addition, I put in individual limit orders or place trailing stops on client positions in an attempt to reduce downside risk. All of these actions are very time consuming, but I feel they are part of what clients are paying me an asset *management* fee for.

4.   What experience do you have?

This question has several nuances to it. The first and most obvious is how long has the advisor been involved in financial planning? There is a big difference between an advisor who has been in the business 5 years and missed the 2008 market collapse and someone who has been in business over 20 years and experienced the stock market swoons of 2000, 2001, 2002 and 2008. Another area of experience would be the advisors area of expertise or specialization closely aligning with your most important need. Third, you may wish to delve into their college major, advanced degrees and industry designations if you haven't already. The downside to experience is another issue you may wish to raise and that is how many years they expect to remain working. If you are 50 years old and would like to work with an advisor through your retirement years, what happens when they decide to retire? Some individual advisors are aligned strongly with a large firm and they might have an arrangement with another advisor at that firm to take over their business when they retire. Others may be in a small firm of three or more advisors and their business continuation plan, like a law firm, is to bring on and train younger advisors to take over their practice when they retire. If you are interviewing an individual advisor who doesn't have a plan on how his practice will transfer to another advisor or firm when he decides to retire, that might be a reason to look elsewhere.

5.   What services do you/your firm provide?

Implicit in this question is also what assistance the advisor will not provide to you. Some advisors focus solely on managing investments. Others provide comprehensive financial planning around retirement, insurance, estate planning and tax planning strategies. Some advisors provide advice for a fee and might recommend how much life insurance you need, but won't help you find the most cost effective policy. Go with someone whose offerings suit your needs.

6. What types of clients do you specialize in working with?
Some financial advisors have a niche and if you have a specific interest – such as charitable giving or socially responsible investments or if you're a newlywed or recently divorced – you'll want to find one that concentrates in that area as well. **Insider Alert!** Just like any good business owner, most advisors will segment their clients into A, B, and C clients. The definition of what an A, B, or C client will differ based upon the types of clients the advisor specializes in. You don't want to be one advisor's C client when another advisor may view you as an A or B client. Unfortunately, in our business many advisors will take on anyone as a client and then ten years later they realize that 20% of their clients are 80% of their revenue and the other 80% of their clients are taking up most of their time. Most advisors I know have between 300 to 500 clients. The cold, hard fact is that you want to align yourself with an advisor who sees you as a valued client, not just another number to add to their book of business.

7. How many clients do you work with?
Technology is a great tool, which helps advisors create efficiencies so that they can bring on more clients and additional assets. This in turn allows the firm to become more profitable. In my opinion, despite technological advances, advisors are still dealing with each client's unique issues and the more clients an advisor has the more divided his attention will be. In some ways this can be alleviated by hiring more staff and using third party investment vehicles so the advisor only spends time on the asset allocation and doesn't have to do his own research and recommendations. The downside is that it can make the relationship with the client less and less personable. My personal opinion is that one advisor cannot be effective with more than 100 clients. They can try, but they will either need to use more and more technology at the exclusion of personal interaction or things may begin to fall through the cracks.

I found it remarkable recently, to hear a commercial on the radio advertising a financial advisor who was almost bragging that they worked with over 500 clients. Is that really a good thing?

8. What is your investment approach?

This is an extremely important question and you want to fully understand the response from the advisor you are interviewing. If you have a strong preference for a particular philosophy, ask the advisor what his or hers is. For instance, you can ask whether they plan to use actively managed funds or passive investments. Throw out any insecurity you may have with your investment knowledge and boldly dig deeper here. Questions you may want to ask include:

- Do you personally invest my money or does someone else?
- If you choose the investments then how do you make your selection?
- Do you believe in market timing, why or why not?
- Do you use active managers or passive managers?
- How did your clients' investment accounts fare in 2008?
- In the future, if the stock market is dropping, like in 2008, would you sell funds and move to cash or hold them all the way down and wait for them to come back? (Buy and Hold)
- What would cause you to recommend changes in my portfolio once we decided on an allocation?
- Is your money invested in the same investments you recommend to clients?

9. How much contact do you have with your clients?

Getting an answer on this question is important because unmet expectations will result in you not being satisfied with your advisor experience. Some advisors streamline their business in an effort to make it as efficient as possible. You will have an initial fact finding meeting, the delivery of a plan with recommendations and then an annual meeting for review. Others may have quarterly check-ins.

I jokingly tell clients that I am extremely inefficient. I customize each client experience for what they are looking for. Many of the senior executives I work with are too busy to meet more than once a year, but they like e-mail updates on a monthly basis. Some of my retired clients like to meet quarterly in person, while others appreciate a phone call. Make sure, up front, that the advisor you choose will meet and contact you in the ways you are looking for.

10. Will I be working only with you or with a team?
Some firms have a team approach, in which the senior advisor will meet with you once a year and the junior planner or administrative assistant will get together with you regularly in between. With other firms you will only meet with the advisor you interview and their assistant will help coordinate administrative issues over the phone or through e-mail. One approach isn't better than another, but this is another case where you don't want to think you will be meeting with your advisor at every review, and then find out someone else from the team is there on his or her behalf.

11. What makes your client experience unique?
If you are meeting with three or more potential advisors, then this is the question that may provide you with their true differentiation. Every financial planner worth working with should tell you that they review your current situation, understand your goals and risk tolerance and then prepare a plan on how to help you achieve your goals. This is basic financial planning 101. Listen to hear if the advisor is truly telling you something unique that no one else has expressed.

Insider Alert: Efficiencies like third-party model portfolios, going paperless, and directing clients to website and other technology platforms are all effective time-saving tools that can be beneficial to an advisor running his business. However, they may also reduce the personalization you might be looking for. For example, broker-dealers may provide approved current topic correspondence which advisors can automatically have sent to clients via e-mail. While this is nice, I like to take the time to put together my own e-letter which reflects the types of investments I am using with clients, changes I am making and why, plus any other thoughts I have on the economy. This is not efficient, but those who receive it provide a lot of positive feedback. It's one thing that makes me unique.

Post meeting summary

After your advisor interviews, it is helpful to do a post meeting summary. If you went in as a husband and wife team, then your post meeting discussion could prove very interesting. Personality is always a great place to start. Did the advisor seem confident? Arrogant? Knowledgeable? Sympathetic? Passionate? Too eager? Did he or she ask insightful questions to get to know you better and seem genuinely interested in you? Other questions you should reflect upon, in no particular order:

- Did you get the feeling the advisor would take anyone on as a client? *Ironically, you should want the advisor to be interviewing you at the same time you are interviewing them. The advisor should want a good fit for their expertise, not just take on another client for the sake of revenue.*
- Were they believable? Did they come across as someone you could trust with your future?
- Did you feel like they would develop a customized plan for you or that you would be just one of the many clients they help?
- What were the unique aspects of each advisor that differentiated them from the others?
- Where/when would future meetings take place? Their office? Your home? Week days? Week nights?
- How would you communicate on a regular basis? E-mail? Phone? Skype? In-person? Mail?
- Was the advisor transparent about all of the ways they are compensated? Was anything unclear?
- Was it a team approach or would you be working with one individual?
- Could you see yourself working with the same firm/individual for the next 10 to 20 plus years?
- What did you like best and worst about the advisor, their office and firm?
- Did they offer all of the services you were looking for?
- Was their technology and reporting a good fit for you?
- Does the advisor work with similar clients to you?
- If you are looking to grow in your own personal knowledge of finances and investing, do you feel they would be a good teacher?

If you discuss all of these questions then one of the advisors should rise to the top. If you've narrowed it down to two, then it's quite alright to have a follow up conversation or e-mail exchange. In this follow up, focus your questions on the 2 or 3 items that are making your decision a difficult one. If your focus is on investments, you may want to ask each advisor to provide you with a sample investment portfolio of what their recommendations might be for you. This could also be helpful in having the advisor explain *all of the fees* associated with that portfolio.

If your focus is on financial planning, have the advisor provide you with the exact fee they would charge for your plan, recommendations and help with implementation. Remember, a plan by itself is useless unless you enact the recommendations to get you to your goals. Make sure you ask the advisor to break down the fees into the following categories:

1. What is the fee for the advice and recommendations? If they respond it is hourly, ask them to estimate the number of hours that will be involved. If it is a flat fee, get the quote for that and how it is paid (up-front, monthly, quarterly, etc.).
2. Ask if there is a separate fee for implementation or if the advisor earns commissions from products implemented through the recommendations. I have seen some advisors continue to charge an hourly rate and make nothing off of products recommended and others charge a flat fee for the year plus commissions.
3. Check to see how your investments might fit into the total fee equation. Beyond the advisor fee, third party fee, and internal fund expenses, I've already discussed, you might have advisors that provide a discount on planning fees if you move a significant amount of assets over to their firm. Others will treat them as two totally separate operations.

Now what?

I was thinking about how I'd like to end our conversation today. It would be vain of me to think I know it all. My mid-life goal is to use the combination of my experiences in the first half, coupled with ongoing learning, to make the second half the best it can be. At the same time, my hope was to provide you with insights I have learned over several decades so that you too can have a more confident retirement and life.

Even if you enjoyed our time and nodded your head that many of the points made sense, I feel it will all be time wasted if you don't incorporate these three items:

Take action now

One day Alice came to a fork in the road and saw a Cheshire cat in a tree.

"Which Road do I take?" she asked.

His response was a question: "Where do you want to go?"

"I don't know," Alice answered.

"Then," said the cat, "it doesn't much matter."

Lewis Carroll, *Alice in Wonderland*

I mentioned it way back in Chapter 2. It is imperative that you take the time to reflect and discuss what it is you want out of life. Then, put it in writing with incremental steps on how you are going to get there. If not, you will wind up with the "Columbus Plan." Christopher Columbus financed his trip on other people's money, sailed off into the ocean not knowing where he was going and didn't know where he was when he got there.

Spontaneity in life is great, but there are certain life issues where you don't want to just wing it. Buying a car or a vacation condo on the beach are both big ticket items, but probably won't have dire consequences if you don't get the best deals. Here are a few issues which can have both life-long consequences and lasting memories. These should take some serious thought.

- **Planning a family.** How many children do you want to have? Do you want to adopt?
- **Raising your children.** How are you going to discipline? What boundaries will you have when they are in middle and high school? What activities will you expose them to – music, sports, languages, community charity, travel, Boy/Girl Scouts, Trail Life, Religion?
- **Education.** Advanced degrees for you and your spouse. Public School, Private School or Home- School for your children.
- **Travel.** Vacations with the family in the United States and abroad. Trips with just your spouse.
- **Where you live.** Many times your vocation dictates this, but there are other times when you have a choice in the matter. This could come through a potential job promotion or lateral move, or through seeking out a new position in a different city, state, or even country.
- **Retirement.** The younger you start the easier it will be later on to reach your goal.

Manage your emotions

During the first week of 2016, the DJIA and S&P 500 indexes dropped over 6%. This was the worst New Year opening week in the history of the indexes. A few days later a writer from a large financial firm put out an article titled: SELL EVERYTHING! This is akin to yelling, "Fire" in a movie theatre.

Three quotes to remember:

"The only thing new in the world is the history you do not know." *Harry S. Truman*
"There is nothing new under the sun." *Ecclesiastes 1:9*
"The four most dangerous words in investing are, this time it's different." *Sir John Templeton*

As discussed previously, the two hardest emotions to keep under control when investing your hard earned money are fear and greed. You must have a strategy for how to control them. If your strategy is having a financial advisor take on that stress for you, then you need to have both trust and patience in their strategy.

There will always be regular pullbacks in the stock market. A -10% decline in the stock market from its high is called a *correction*. If it does so in one day, that is a *crash*. And when the stock market drops -20% or more from its high, that signifies a bear market. From 1900 through 2013, there were 123 corrections (about one per year) and 32 bear markets (one every 3.5 years)[1], but two facts remain. First, if you retire at age 60-65, and are a non-smoker, there is a high probability that either you or your spouse will live another 30 years. Second, the cost of living over a 30 year period rises approximately 2.5 times. Therefore hiding your money under a mattress with a 0% return, in a guaranteed treasury or bank account with little interest earned, or even investing in other fixed income investments earning less than 3% return is not a good option.

From history, we know that since the beginning of the stock market there has never been a 30 year period where you would have lost money from the starting point to the ending point. In addition, bear markets are usually shorter than bull markets. Despite the pullbacks, the S&P 500 has returned an average of 9.9% a year, including dividends, from 1900 through 2013.[2] So, instead of focusing on the idea of investing in "the market," which sounds like a big, black box, think of it as putting your money into the American and world companies that you patronize every day.

You want your money to outlive you. You don't want to outlive your money. To manage your emotions, it may help to segment your retirement investments into two accounts. One account is your less volatile, fixed income investments. This is the place you go to first with your Required Minimum Distributions (RMD) if equities are down. The other account has your stock investments that you can allow time to recover after a pull back. From a historical and mathematical standpoint, it makes senses to have equities in your portfolio for your entire life. So whether you are investing on your own or using an advisor, it is important to learn how best to cope with the emotions of fear and greed that might disrupt your retirement plans.

If you read or listen to the headlines in your favorite newspaper, website, or cable news show, you will be able to find opposing economic predictions on a daily basis. I like the quote from John Kenneth Galbraith, a U.S. Administrator & Economist, who said:

"The only function of economic forecasting is to make astrology look respectable."

Are there ways to try and avoid bear markets or at least soften the blow without trying to time the market? I believe so and addressed that issue back in Chapter Nine.

Stay Positive

I am naturally a positive person. My wife tends to be more of a realist. That can be a good thing to balance one another out. When I forecast business projections and various opportunities, I will typically aim high by making positive assumptions. While my wife is not a "Debbie Downer," she will insightfully ask, "what if" questions. These are the types of issues that can surface and disrupt your planning, like ones we discussed in Chapters Four and Five.

One of my favorite military quotes on having a positive outlook comes from General Craton Abrams, at the Battle of the Bulge, during World War 2, when he addresses his men.

"For the first time in the history of this campaign we are surrounded on the East, West, North and South. We can now attack the enemy in all directions."

Now that's a positive attitude!

Remember that no matter what life may send your way, there is always hope. Ignoring problems because you are embarrassed by decisions you've made in the past is not the answer. And neither is putting off the hard decisions on how to fix them. I have a framed cartoon in my office of a potential client sitting down in front of a financial advisor. His opening statement is:

"I'm retiring next week and haven't save a dime. Now's your chance to become a legend."

While I like to think I'm good at my job, I'm not that good. The earlier you address an issue the better off you will be. So take action now, manage your emotions, and be positive!

To get the latest information and updates on THE ONE THING, go to www.theonething.one

You can also e-mail Eric directly at eric@theonething.one

APPENDIX

Questions and statements for fathers to discuss with boys who want to date their daughters.

From Chapter Two

1. What does dating mean to you?
2. You and I both know my daughter is beautiful. What other things attract you to her?
3. I am responsible for my daughter's physical and emotional well-being. When she is with you, I am holding you accountable for that.
4. Whether you text, e-mail, message, FaceTime, chats or call on the phone, assume that I am viewing it or listening and you will be okay.
5. Whether you date my daughter once or fifty times, I want you to treat her like you would want someone to treat your future wife.
6. I expect you to respect my daughter's purity. Anything below the neck and above the knees is off-limits.
7. If you ever get in any situation where you are uncomfortable or need any kind of help, I want you to call immediately.
8. Personal interest questions are great. Do you participate in any sports or clubs? What's your favorite subject in school? Do you know what you would like to do after high school?
9. Where are you at on your spiritual journey?
10. Bonus statement (not required): I typically ended our meal discussion by looking the young man in the eyes and stating, "As you know I am very concerned about my daughter's well-being. If you make her cry… I am going to make you cry."

Ask if he has any questions or needs anything clarified. Thank him for coming to speak with you. At that point, you can give him permission to take out your daughter. Or if you have any reservations you can buy yourself some time by saying you'll think over the conversation and get back to him with an answer.

REFERENCES

Chapter 1
1   Use of *City Slickers* movie excerpt used with permission from Warner Bros. Entertainment Inc. June 21, 2016.

Chapter 2
1. Zig Ziglar quote use with permission, June 10, 2016, Ziglar.com.

2. CFP Board's Standards of Professional Conduct Copyright ©2016, Certified Financial Planner Board of Standards, Inc. All rights reserved. Used with permission."

3. Rainey, Dennis and Barbara. *Parenting Today's Adolescent.* Plano: Thomas Nelson, 2002. Print.

4. Rainey, Dennis. *Interviewing your Daughter's Date: 30 Minutes Man-To-Man.* Little Rock: Family Life Publishing. 2012. Print.

Chapter 3
1. Use of *Meet the Parents* movie excerpt used with permission from Universal Studios, July 29, 2016.

Chapter 4
1. Colson, Charles. From a speech delivered by Charls Colson at the National Religious Broadcasters Convention 2/84 and reported in *Religious Broad- casting* 3/84

Chapter 8

1. Floyd, Elaine. (2007) *"Radical Thoughts on Asset Allocation,"* working paper.

2. Cloonan, James B. "Popular Allocation Approaches Put the Cart Before the Horse." *AAII Journal.* Sep. 2002.

3. Graham, Benjamin. *The Intelligent Investor.* Benjamin Graham. 1949. Print.

4. Fisher, Philip. *Common Stocks and Uncommon Profits.* Harper & Brothers. New York City: 1960. Print.

5. Fisher, Lawrance., Lorie, James H. "Some Studies of Variability of Returns on Investments in Common Stocks," *The Journal of Business,* Vol. 43, No. 2 (1970): 99-134. 3 Apr. 1970.

Chapter 9

1. S&P 500 Index Returns and Permanent Portfolio Mutual Fund (PRPFX) – Morningstar Research.

2. Biller, Mark. "Dynamic Asset Allocation: An Investing Strategy for the Risk-Averse," *Sound Mind Investing,* (2012): Dec. 24, 2012.

3. Ibid.

4. Vomund, David. *ETF Trading Strategies Revealed.* Marketplace Books. Columbia: 2006. Print.

5. Antonacci, Gary. *Dual Momentum Investing – An Innovative Strategy for Higher Returns with Lower Risk.* Mcgraw Hill. New York City: 2015. Print.

6. Ibid.

7. Biller, Mark. "Beyond The Passive Vs. Active Investing Debate: SMI Uses Both," *Sound Mind Investing*, (2016): Aug. 26, 2016.

Chapter 10

1. https://financialaid.fsu.edu/apply/cost_ungrad.html

2. http://www.sc.edu/apply/cost_tuition_financial_aid/

3. Research Center, "Signature Report 6: Completing College: A National View of Student Attainment Rates – Fall 2007 Cohort," *National Student Clearinghouse Research Center*, (2013): Dec. 15, 2013.

4. Perry, Mark J. "The college textbook bubble and how the 'open educational resources' movement is going up against the textbook cartel," *AEI*, (2012): Dec. 24, 2012.

5. Kurtzleben, Daniel, "How Your Textbook Dollars Are Divvied Up," *U.S. News & World Report*, (2012): Aug. 28, 2012.

6. http://www.usna.edu/Admissions/index.php

Chapter 12

1. Ozawa, Nancy. "More than 12 Million Identity Fraud Victims in 2012 According to Latest Javelin Strategy & Research Report," *Javelin*, (2013): Feb. 20, 2013.

Chapter 14

1. Reinhold, Eric J. "10 Things Financial Advisors Don't Want You to Know," *Sound Mind Investing*, (2001): August 2001.

Summary

1. Mullaney, Tim, "8 things you need to know about bear markets," *CNBC and Ned Davis Research*, (2015) Aug 24, 2015.

2. Ibid.

Bible References – unless otherwise noted all scriptures are from the New International Version.

The Holy Bible, New International Version. Grand Rapids: Zondervan House, 1984. Print.

The Holy Bible, New American Standard Bible. La Habra: Foundation Publications, 1997. Print.

Peterson, Eugene, *The Message: The Bible in Contemporary Language*. Colorado Springs: NavPress, 2016. Print.

www.ingramcontent.com/pod-product-compliance
Lightning Source LLC
Chambersburg PA
CBHW060043210326
41520CB00009B/1247